PRAISE FOR
SURRENDER

"John Stanley is a dynamic leader with a heart, message, and delivery style that is perfect for speaking to both young and old on how to live life to its fullest as a committed follower of Christ. John's writing is entertaining, fun, insightful, and full of wisdom far beyond his years. If you're longing to be inspired, encouraged, and motivated to grow in your faith, then buy this book. You will be blessed!"

—Robin Creasman
Keynote Speaker (Personal development, leadership, motivation)

"John and his wife, Sarah, have had more than their share of 'white water' in their young lives. This has provided ample real-life opportunities to live out true surrender. Join John as he shares honest, thought-provoking insight into his journey with his Savior. You will appreciate the wise, candid lessons he has learned along the way and value his encouraging words."

—Jeremy Good
Worship Pastor, Cornerstone Community Bible Church
Rosenberg, TX

"A clearly focused examination of every pilgrim's journey. Everyone who is looking to know 'how to get through it' with peace and victory must read *Surrender!*"

—Dr. Roy Hayes
President and Artistic Director, True North Presents

D1520351

"John Stanley is among the young rising leaders in the body of Christ today who give joy and hope to the older generation—among whom age and time position me. John has the zest of the young, but wisdom from the rich experience and learning he's already gained. Youthful passion and mature wisdom combine to make this book rich in orthodoxy (truth) and orthopraxy (application)."

—Wallace Henley
Author of *God and Churchill* and *Globequake*
Columnist, *Christian Post*

"John Stanley takes us on a ride of hope, surrender, and promise as he compares a gutsy white-water rafting trip from his youth to the lessons of life. It's on this river that he learns to surrender to the commands of the guide, pointing us to the only true Guide: Jesus Christ. Through the backdrop of rapids, paddles, and intense navigation, he weaves an invitation to prayer and belief. With engaging style, Stanley shares his life stories, leaving the imprint of a wild river that takes us to a breaking point, only to be rescued by a Savior wild with love."

—Gari Meacham
Author of *Watershed Moments* and *Spirit Hunger*

"To surrender can give the impression of having one's hands up and weapons down—conquered and lost. But in John Stanley's book, *Surrender*, we learn that surrender is the path to life, hope, peace, and freedom. John's warm conversational style and solid biblical insights guide us through the rapids of life by focusing our attention on our Guide instead of on ourselves. Use this book as a gift to friends who need hope, and as a gift to yourself in your walk with Christ."

—Brad Mitchell
President, Build Your Marriage

"This is a refreshing book by John Stanley. He has provided a creative and inspiring spiritual resource for readers of all ages. John has focused on the important truth of surrendering one's life to God as the first priority for success and true happiness. He uses a childhood experience of white-water rafting to capture the reader's attention and to lead into meaningful spiritual applications. He applies the lessons learned to life's fears and hurts. He moves from the self-glorifying mentality in today's culture and context, which will ultimately bring failure, to a total dependence on God for all of life. Of special value, this book provides some inspiring, heartwarming illustrations of persons moving beyond tragedy, allowing God to take control of their lives in total dependence. I am delighted to recommend this volume for personal devotional reading and for use in small group studies in churches."

—Dr. Bernie Spooner
Associate Dean/Professor, Dallas Baptist University
Chair of the Commission on Theological Education and Leadership
Formation, Baptist World Alliance

"John's sheer honesty and candor may well drive you to the realization that God is very near, and He desires to reveal Himself to you. John does a tremendous job of connecting the profound with the practical in such a way that inspires you to consider how God is at work in your own life and how you should respond to Him."

—Chris Stanley
Minister of Adults, West Conroe Baptist Church, Conroe, TX

"*Surrender* is a book that illuminates your heart with joy, while empowering your spirit onward in a journey of relentless initiative and unwavering determination toward Christ—to surrender your fears so you may win the fight like Gideon, to surrender your selfish ambitions to serve and protect your family, and to surrender your heart for kingdom work and everlasting life. Read it, and then read it again."

—Matt Stanley
President and CEO, Sundance Memory Care

"It may not always be a popular message, but surrender is at the heart of the Christian journey. Both salvation and sanctification hinge on it. What a joy to see a warm, honest, and transparent book from John Stanley taking dead aim at surrender—just as our Lord often did. Filled with personal stories and life lessons, and balanced between lighthearted and serious, Stanley writes like a good friend dialoguing with you about what really matters. This book has the capacity to move you to transformation."

—Dr. Peter Swann
Lead Pastor, Hope Church
Executive Director, Every Village, Houston, TX

"John Stanley's book, *Surrender*, is insightful, powerful, and inspiring. A must-read for anyone wanting to be all that God created them to be with a sense of adventure, purpose, and destiny."

—Zoro
World-renowned drummer for Lenny Kravitz
Motivational speaker
Author of *The Big Gig*

SURRENDER

LEARNING TO NAVIGATE LIFE'S DEEP
WATERS WITH CHRIST AS YOUR GUIDE

JOHN STANLEY

Fort Washington, PA 19034

Surrender
Published by CLC Publications

U.S.A.
P.O. Box 1449, Fort Washington, PA 19034

UNITED KINGDOM
CLC International (UK)
Unit 5, Glendale Avenue, Sandycroft, Flintshire, CH5 2QP

ISBN (paperback): 978-1-61958-284-2
ISBN (e-book): 978-1-61958-285-9

Cover design by Mitch Bolton.

DEDICATION

To my wife, Sarah, the most amazing, God-fearing, loving, gentle, patient, and beautiful woman in my life. You are an inspiration that brings a brilliant, hopeful light to so many. Watching you live out surrender in your every waking moment teaches me so much. I love you more than words can say. You are my hero and my most cherished love. I'm so grateful for you!

To my two wonderful and gifted kiddos. I pray, as your father, that surrender is lived out before you with a joyful expectation that deepens your faith in a very real way. There are no greater arms that can hold you than those of Christ Jesus. May you grow intimately linked with Him in the amazing future set before you. I love you, and I am so grateful for you and so proud of you. I pray that God's great joy and laughter will overwhelm you daily, so that you may live abundantly in His peace as you intentionally pursue surrender.

ACKNOWLEDGMENTS

As a musician, I have learned the great value of a team. A team works together through individual imperfections and builds upon each other's strengths, bringing together a collaborative effort with impact and inspiration. This book would not even be readable without the help of so many. Where to even start? My gratitude for the individuals mentioned is beyond words of explanation. You helped take something so raw and unpolished and have given it the best possible opportunity to be read. Thank you, thank you, thank you!

To my editors, Tracey Michae'l Lewis-Giggetts and Natalie Cohen. Your honesty was refreshing. You treated this book like it was your own, and for that I am deeply grateful. Thank you for your cautious critiques and time.

To the CLC publishing team. I'm honored that you even took the chance. Your patience with me has been encouraging and so kind. A giant salute to Dave Almack, Erika Cobb, and Yuko Momose.

Bob Kelly, you turned this around. The time and effort you gave for this work and the patience you demonstrated was profound. I'm so grateful for you and the gifts God has given you. Words fall short.

To my agent, Gary Foster. Thank you for working with me and working so hard for this book. You gave much-needed wisdom throughout this process and helped guide me through some unclear water. Because of you this project was moved into existence. I'm greatly appreciative!

To those who in great degrees of kindness and sacrifice offered feedback, direction, and encouragement as this process moved forward. I could not have done this without you. Some big thanks are in order for Gary Thomas, Gari Meacham, Drew Daniels, Alli Sepulveda, Larry Harrison, Dr. Bernie Spooner, Dr. Danny Havard, Dr. Peter Swann, Dr. James R. DeLoach, Wallace Henley, Andrew Nix, Brad Mitchell, Dave Riggle, and Zoro the Drummer.

A special acknowledgment to Second Baptist Church. The message of surrender in Christ is given so clearly every week without hesitation. To God be the glory for what He is doing in and throughout His people at Second and across the world. Great things are to come as we continue to lift up Jesus and make Him known!

And to my family. Dad, Mom, Matt, and Chris. Man, have we lived life together or what?! The years we spent being navigated through treacherous water, and at times barely making it through. I'm so grateful for our life together and I've learned so much from all of you. Love, grace, forgiveness, hope in unrelenting dark places, relentless initiative, thriving as we exist within the call of God—all while Jesus remained at the center and kept us grounded through it all. Your faith and devotion inspire me. I'm so glad to have been born into our family which in turn led me into the family of God.

Grace and peace to you all.

CONTENTS

PROLOGUE

We live in interesting times to say the least—politically, economically, socially, environmentally, and technologically. Trends are changing and evolving at such a perplexing rate, that it can be hard to keep up with "what's new." Environmentally, we're seeing weather patterns develop that extend to extremes—from virtually incomprehensible flooding, earthquakes, wildfires, and rising temperatures, to exceptionally cold weather creating freezing conditions that haven't been experienced in some regions of the earth in over two decades. Politically, it seems our world is in a constant state of negotiations for peace. Global leaders fight for positions of dominance as mankind watches from afar, fearful of what the outcome might be. Words like *peace*, *harmony*, and *reconciliation* are consistently discussed across almost every media platform, but the realization of such order is very distant.

The global economy continues to be in a state of uncertainty. Individual and corporate financial vulnerabilities are mounting which can cause a weakness in possible growth. While there is hope projected for a universal economic boost, its sustainability is questionable.

Socially, we live in a day where common sense, wisdom, truth, conviction, and the discernment to correctly and respectively state our convictions seem lost. Decency and reverence have been replaced by physical acts and communication of radical, unkind, and evil extremes. A mature sense of balance and response dictated by love has seemingly been replaced by reactionary outbursts that continually create a divide rather than unify.

We live in a world that longs for peace, but screaming "PEACE!" from the rafters isn't solving the problem. Passionate cries filled with anger, bitterness, and vengeful spite, aimed toward individuals who we've become convinced are dismantling our worldview, is not ushering in a lasting solution. Soon we come to find that inevitably another "wrong" will occur, and the cycle starts all over again.

Core values are changing at a rapid pace. It feels as if we are being tossed around by a raging ocean tide, and the mature response to "agree to disagree" has all but been washed away. We'd rather leave our emotions and feelings unchecked if someone challenges our opinion or belief—especially when it comes to an ideology we value and hold dear.

In this day and age, social media dominates our attention and has become a consuming source of influence, leading us to think that the perception and opinion of others, in one way or another, is what sets our standard of truth. How we are perceived is where we find the foundation of our acceptance. Common sense has lost its measure of worth, and absolute truth is being pushed to the side.

As these ever-evolving trends and behaviors have become all the more prevalent in our society, we've seen an increase in fear, anxiety, frustration, anger, and even hate. Look around. Look into the world that surrounds you. Is peace prevailing? The more everyone becomes righteous in their own eyes, the more such self-driven and self-gratifying pride becomes a dividing line. If peace and unity are the goals of humanity, we are failing.

Is there hope? Is there hope for real transformation? As the people of God, what can we do about it? As Christ followers are we reflecting a current of change within our culture? Are we portraying something different? Have we intentionally set ourselves apart? What is our standard of truth? Are we living out the commandment given in Colossians 3:12 when it says, "So, as those who have been chosen of God, holy and beloved, put on a heart of compassion, kindness, humility, gentleness and patience"?

Or, as the people of God, have we allowed our culture to define us, individually and collectively? In regards to what we value, has fame and popular perception become an unintentional pursuit and platform within the body of Christ?

Concerning foundational and biblical truth, have we become fearful of teaching and holding to the standards that God has ordained and laid forth by the authority of His word? Or have we become more concerned with being socially acceptable and likable—and, as some mistakenly mark it, *relatable*? And the larger question at heart: Have we ultimately allowed ourselves to come under the authority of man rather than that of God?

The reality of surrender in our lives comes down to that one question. Man or God? It's literally a question of authority. We're all surrendered to something. We've all raised the white flag and given into a ruling, authoritative set of thoughts, beliefs, and behaviors that are defining us and defining the influence we have on those around us.

Those thoughts and beliefs reveal where we find our worth. They reveal the authentic motives behind our pursuits. They uncover the truth of what or who we really value. Maybe some of us have forgotten that in due time we'll be held accountable for what we've worked to construct.

Individually, we need to ask ourselves: To whom or to what are we surrendered? Who we are individually works to make up the church as a whole collectively. So, our individual commitments of our time and our resources ultimately determine how the church will operate. The priorities that are lived out in our waking moments are laying the foundation of our impact in society as single and communal disciples of Christ. As followers of Jesus, His word is our authority and we are to surrender to His commands. God before man.

When writing for an orchestra, the solitary goal of a composer is to take every individual instrument and bring the different voices together to create a (hopefully) beautiful song. Each voice has a place, but there will be one voice that soars above all the others if the composition is written correctly. That voice is the melody. The melody and the instrument or instruments that carry the melody take center stage, while the rest of the orchestra works together to gloriously reveal the beauty of the series of notes that need to be heard.

As a composition begins to build in intensity and all the voices start working together, it can be easy for the melody to get lost. So, written within the music are specific dynamics for each instrument. In other words, the instruments are prioritized within an authority structure. The authority that sets the standard of each orchestral voicing is the melody. Without the melody, all the other notes become a parade of sound without direction. Melody comes before harmony.

As followers of Jesus, obedience to God, His word, and His kingdom comes first. As is stated in Matthew 6:33, "But seek first His kingdom and His righteousness."

This is our aim in real surrender. In God's righteousness we find peace (see Isa. 32:17) and are no longer conformed to the pattern of this world (see Rom. 12:2). We find that we are set apart.

To influence the world around us, God's authority must rule in our hearts. He is the melody to our song. To individually come under God's authority brings unity. And much like the different instruments of an orchestra, in unity there's still diversity, freedom, and power.[1] The parts of the body of Christ don't have the same appearance or function, but they are all significant, have a need, are linked together, and work toward the same goal. In the church, there are purposes for each member—designed for the function of the body as guided by the head, which is Christ. They work together and work in harmony with the creative purpose of God the Father.

Therefore we have a united purpose. The purpose is maturity in Christ, while the ultimate goal of being is to be Christlike. This is the primary pursuit and equipping nature of surrender. The more we possess the character and mind of Jesus, the more the unity of the Spirit will be experienced—and thus the more God's peace will abound in our hearts, in our lives, and in our sphere of influence in the world. This is surrender.

—John Stanley

ONE

A BIG RAFT, SOME WHITE WATER, AND ONE FREAKED OUT LITTLE KID

My mom and dad are great parents—supportive, encouraging, and inspiring. They gave me strong spiritual guidance as a child and taught me how to be creative. Our occasional family trips doubled as a "life lesson." Whether we went camping, hiking, hunting, or on road trips, my parents made sure each adventure or activity taught us a valuable lesson regarding the truths of life and the purpose of our existence. One of those excursions was to the Ocoee River in Tennessee. I survived the first of many traumatic life experiences while I was on that trip.

At age twelve, I was a little guy with not much "meat on the bones," as my grandfather would say. I weighed about seventy pounds, maybe a little less. Combine that with a huge, bouncy rubber raft; a big, yellow paddle taller than I was; and some even bigger white-water rapids and, well, you get the picture. It was shaping up to be a "see ya later" kind of ride.

We pulled into the dusty, rocky parking lot of a local rafting company headquartered in a rustic log cabin deep in the woods, about five miles from the Ocoee River. We piled out of our maroon minivan and saw the river guides who, despite living on a river for a whole summer, were surprisingly clean cut. The college- and adult-aged men had a clean shave, washed clothing that wasn't faded or torn, and hair that had recently been cut—a seemingly good, grounded, and acceptable group.

Except for one. In my child mind, he looked like a serial killer. He had a good bit of scruff on his face and long, greasy, curly brown hair that hung just below his shoulders. I was certain it hadn't been washed since his childhood. He was a bigger man, standing tall at about 6'3" with tree-trunk legs and muscular, beefed-up arms. To me, he looked scary as all get out. This guy was someone you're taught to run away from when you're twelve years old, not someone you'd entrust your life to.

Well, wouldn't you know it? We ended up with that guy as our guide.

Now at twelve, my prayer life was clearly growing. Prayers that would be considered "begging" were few and far between. Yet the moment I found out he was our guide and our only chance of survival, I pleaded to God in every way to be released from the nightmare that had just begun. But sometimes, no matter how hard we beg, there's a purpose for why we are where we are. In hindsight, I think God probably smiled, maybe even laughed a little and said, "You'll be fine." Did I feel that way? Nope.

Then it got worse.

We loaded onto the bus and made our way down some curvy, tar-paved roads that led to the river. The driver parked and opened the doors, and we began to file out. I took one look at the watercourse ahead and my stomach dropped to my feet. I thought, *We were brought here to die.* My parents have thought it all through. They have the killer, they have the whitewater, and death is sure to follow. Great "lesson," Mom and Dad. Thanks a lot. We love you, too!

Little did I know it would turn out fine, but not until we finished the scariest ride of my life. Everything in between the start and finish line of this little journey is still unnerving when I think back through it all. But in the midst of my personal turmoil, the lesson had already begun.

So there we were, standing up to our knees in the frigid water. I was just trying to catch my breath and calm myself down as horrid thoughts raced through my mind. What was going to happen to us? As the self-absorbed tween, I also wondered, what is going to happen to me? How long will it take for me to fly out of the raft and drown? I watched the white-water caps slam against the rocks as the river curved a long path to what seemed like certain doom. I was done for.

It didn't look like fun. In fact, it seemed evil. Yet there my parents stood with huge smiles across their faces. My dad was "livin' it up!" as he would say on virtually any adventurous journey. As I stood with my eyes locked on the terror before me, I made sure my life jacket was secure, my helmet was fastened, and the paddle grips were in the right place. Then I took a deep breath and climbed aboard the raft.

Now because I didn't weigh much, I was put in the back. Heavier people were placed in the front to help keep the raft from flipping front to back when we hit harder rapids, like those ranked class V. I attempted to secure my feet in the grips underneath the seating in front of me, though I didn't feel it would do much good. In my mind, placing such a little guy in the back of the raft didn't seem to be a great idea. With one unsteady bounce, I could shoot up and out like a cannonball on some kind of raging rant of destruction.

Oh, and the worst part? The "killer guide man" who was scarier than anyone I'd ever seen sat right behind me. His booming voice could have caused anyone to freeze so naturally, when we started moving down the river and he screamed, "DIG!" I froze. It evidently caught his attention that I was doing nothing, so he calmly leaned into my ear and politely said in that scruffy tone, "When I tell you to dig, boy, you dig. Got it?" Now, I don't know about you, but when someone who looks like he could snap you into kindling leans into your little ear and commands you do what he says, you either pee your pants or you dig. I chose the latter.

As I attempted the first of many failed "digs" in my panicked state, my paddle was barely reaching the water. So my dig, as it was supposed to be, was nothing more than a dip. Still, terrorized and humiliated as I was, I screamed at everyone else at the top of my lungs to "DIG GUYS!" Later, as we made it farther down the river, I'm sure someone in our family wanted to put me out of my misery.

As we continued the terror ride, our guide gave strong directives through every twist and turn. If they weren't followed to the detail or with the necessary tenacity, he made it crystal clear that we would certainly be in some big trouble. All were doing their part, pulling their weight, except me. I was petrified.

As we approached one of the larger rapids, a few photographers hired by the rafting company perched themselves on the rocks to take pictures of the rafters—you know, so everyone could remember the day they almost met their Maker. Naturally, being the performer I am, I smiled at the cameras and completely ignored our current situation. The picture of our crew details the irony: Everyone else is fighting to make sure they survive, gripping their paddles, faces disheveled as they look steadfastly at the river path ahead. And then there's me, smiling with my paddle not even close to the water. It looks like I was photoshopped or something. Remember the song lyrics, "One of these things is not like the other"? I was that thing.

By the gracious hand of God, we made it down the river. Yes, we survived and finally arrived at our destination. I do believe it was one of the happiest moments of my life. As we gathered on the bus and began to head back, my parents asked me and my brother, "So what did you guys learn about life from that river ride?" I wanted to answer cleverly, "How to die." Before the words could escape my mouth, my parents laid out their reasoning, plain and simple. Their words were etched in my mind and are still with me to this day: "It's all about surrender."

TWO

A LESSON IN SURRENDER

I am the vine, you are the branches . . . for apart from Me you can do nothing.

John 15:5

As we made our way back to headquarters, my parents began to explain what they were trying to teach us. The lesson was something like this: Life is like a river and you will come up against a variety of waters. You will have your calm stretches, your small bumps, and your raging rapids. It's your choice how you navigate them. On the white-water course, we had a guide. Our surrender to his commands ensured we would reach the right destination safely and securely. As Christians, our guide is Christ. He gives us instructions and we have a choice to either trust and obey, or go on our own way. To guarantee we reach the destination He has for us, we must surrender to His lead and guidance.

That's a pretty staunch and profound lesson for a twelve-year-old kid. It's one I haven't forgotten, and to be truthful, I still struggle with it. When I come to a season of the unknown and I'm literally walking by faith, it can be hard to trust in the navigation of my Savior. When I see a family member going through a particularly hard season, I can easily get angry with God and push aside the truth of His sovereignty, grace, and unparalleled provision.

Because I can be so self-absorbed, I often lose focus of God's great love and forget to simply say "thank you!" There are so many things that I can take for granted every single day. The provisions of food, clothes, shoes, shelter, and transportation. The fact that we have clean drinking water where we live, and electricity to provide power for our needs and wants. As a musician, it's easy to take for granted the fact that I can hear, that I can see the sheet music in front of my eyes, that am able to read it and comprehend the notations. It's been easy to spiritually take steps backward and become inwardly driven and motivated because I've become singularly focused on me and my surroundings. There have been times when I've thrown fits or have become radically discouraged because my prayers aren't answered the way I'd like them to be.

Like the time when I failed my first piano jury as a freshman in college. God didn't give the professors grace and mercy to pass me like I had asked, even though I was the one who didn't prepare and couldn't play a darn thing. Or one of the times I lied to my parents and asked God that I not get caught, although I deserved to, and I needed the consequences in order to learn.

John, come on, you might be thinking. *In those examples, you brought the repercussions on yourself!*

Okay then, let's venture into deeper waters.

In my early teenage years, I vividly remember pleading with God to spare my best friend's life after he was badly injured in a terrible car wreck. Instead of experiencing God's healing, my friend passed away. In the first years of my marriage, I prayed one morning that during the day, God would bring a special blessing to my wife and me and our unity together. Instead of bringing joy, appreciation, and respect like I had hoped, tension and frustration were stirred up to such a degree that same day that my wife left the house and drove away for quite a few hours. And for the here and now, there have been many years of consistent prayer for the complete healing of my wife as she continues to deal with persistent pain. However, a struggle still exists because pain still exists to a certain extent. In each of these circumstances, there have been times during prayer that I've thrown my hands up the air and said, "What good is this?!"

In these seasons, trusting in the leading of Christ is difficult. It can be easy to be swept away by the current and not hold fast to the truth and navigation of our Guide. It can get really tough to remain with Him. Yet as we follow Christ, a key command is made clear in John 15:4 when Jesus says, "Abide in me." The word *abide* in this context means "to stay, continue, dwell, endure, and remain."[1] In this one statement, Christ defines a disciple's journey. We're to "remain in Him or with Him" and stay the course.

All of this is built on the foundation of a loving and intimate relationship which blossoms as we intentionally create time to communicate with our Savior and heavenly Father. This is what begins to build trust between us and our Creator. It's one thing to say we trust God, but it's another thing entirely for Him to trust us. I'm not talking about public appearances at church, worship events, or Bible study. Yes, community is a necessity. However, to nurture a relationship of total trust, we must purposefully pursue times in which we're alone with God. This is where surrender begins.

A marriage cannot grow unless the man and woman deliberately pursue one another and cherish the one-on-one relationship. A parent will not bond with their child unless that mother or father invests the time needed to cultivate a precious and profound one-on-one connection. Finding time to be alone with our Creator is the most vital aspect of expectantly living in total abandon and trust with Him. This is where the essential depth of our relationship with God occurs.

The family of God, united by the blood of Christ, is a great encouragement to our growth and there are many ways to stay connected within such a framework. We can join a local Bible-believing and teaching church. We can get involved in that community. We must not merely be spectators. In church community, we can surround ourselves with other Christians who will encourage and vow to walk with us in our faith. They'll keep us accountable in our lifestyle and the decisions we make. It's wise to connect with other believers and mentors who help to cultivate our personal relationship with Christ and provide uplifting support. More importantly, we must work every day in our one-on-one relationship with our Guide. This takes discipline. To hear and correctly understand the leading of Jesus, we must strive to be intimately connected with Him. We do this by absorbing the Bible through study and being active in prayer daily. We should pursue such disciplines with intentionality.

I have seen this truth amplified since I've been married and had children. Marriage truly redefines our lives, our priorities, and our pursuits. The heaviness of the responsibility of marriage hit me particularly hard during our engagement. I literally lost forty pounds in four months. By our wedding day, the tux I had been fitted for weeks after I proposed hung from my body like loose rags. After Sarah and I said our vows and cemented the covenant of marriage between us and God, the pressure of assuming the responsibility of being a husband and the spiritual leader and provider of a home was daunting.

When fatherhood came around, well, I'm not sure I was exactly sane for the first few months after our daughter was born. The burden I felt to be a good father was mentally and spiritually exhausting. I knew beyond a shadow of a doubt that I would mess up, but the responsibility of a little girl and the known bond between a daughter and father—man alive, that was a lot to take in! Then, with the birth of our son and the amazing responsibility a father has to his boy, the pressure hit me all over again. In both of those new experiences, I felt that in order to end strong, I had to start strong, and I had no clue what I was doing as a husband or a father. I knew my relationship with the Lord would be absolutely critical and foundational in my new roles. After actually living within the framework of these disciplines, it has proved to be vital.

I have found that as my relationship with the Lord grows, I grow in discernment and wisdom. This greatly impacts how I make tough life decisions. It also influences my prayer life—to know how to pray, and who and what to pray for—and it also helps me to clearly recognize which opportunities are from God and which opportunities are not.

A PERSONAL STORY

When my wife and I were first engaged, we enrolled in a marriage class at our church. One of the first questions we encountered through the curriculum was: Have you discussed how many children you would like to have? If so, have you discussed their names? What would you like to name your son(s)? What would you like to name your daughter(s)?

We were encouraged to write down our responses without looking at each other's papers. After we wrote down our answers, we turned to share. We had discussed children and had discussed that we'd like to have a boy and a girl, but we had never discussed names. On our papers, we had both written the same name for a boy. We thought that was a pretty neat confirmation. I didn't know it at the time, but Sarah had clung to a hopeful promise that God had given her regarding a son being born of that name.

We were absolutely overjoyed when our daughter came into the world. The road to pregnancy had been tough (more on this in chapter 6), but our little girl was living proof that God can reverse the circumstances of His children. About a year and half after she was born, God began to move in our hearts and planted the desire for another child. But because of the journey to our first pregnancy, we didn't know what to expect with our second or if having a second child would even be possible. After watching my wife struggle through the first pregnancy, I was having trouble with the thought of going through all of that again. A God-ordained purpose of a husband is to be a protector and provider of his family. So naturally, I wanted to protect my wife from going through such a similar struggle.

Thinking through this one morning in prayer, I simply laid an honest request before the Lord. I asked Him what exactly I should pray for Sarah and the new little one He had put on our hearts. This was one of the first times I felt I had ever heard God's voice so clearly. I wrote down: Pray for a son.

Before I could ask for specifics, a list of details and attributes regarding his personality and physicality came to my mind, so I wrote those down as well. I then began praying specifically for a son and who God would make him to be. About a month and half later, Sarah revealed to me that she was pregnant and we soon found out we were having a boy. I did not share with Sarah what God had revealed until much later down the road and to this day, when we recall the story and look over what I had written down that morning, we are still in awe. Our son precisely fits that description, right down to the specifics of his personality and physical attributes.

Husbands and fathers are called to be spiritual leaders and enter the throne room of heaven to serve our families and lavishly love them with the love of Christ. Jesus petitions for us, so we must do the same for our wives and children every day. This links us intimately with our Creator and allows us to grow a deeper relationship with Him that can enable us to see what He sees. I now realize that to be fully effective in our purpose, whatever role God calls us into, this truth must take root. It's the foundation of our very existence. It clearly connects us to God's great plan of adventure for us, our family, our friends, and those in our realm of influence. We're not fully capable on our own to work and bear fruit that's wholly acceptable and pleasing to God unless this truth remains consistent in our thoughts, actions, and pursuits.

Where are you on this "river" journey called life? Are you abiding in Christ or are you being persuaded by everything around you that says, "just do your own thing; follow your heart's desire"? It's saddening to see our society gravitate to this mind-set of "just do what you feel as long as you don't hurt anyone." As Luke 16:15 points out, not every desire is legitimate: "For that which is highly esteemed among men is detestable in the sight of God." Children live on feeling. Adults should be aware of the wisdom of common sense and solid truth.

Surrender to God requires a total abandonment of what we think is best in order to follow the lead of the One who knows what's best. If you believe this, then be encouraged: You are off to a great start! But we must put steps to our faith. Surrendered territory can sometimes look dangerous, risky, scary, and unpredictable. And it's in those places we find that moving forward is where the struggle begins.

THE SPIRIT OF FEAR

God has given us an emotion that puts flags up when we see a threat or feel we are in danger. It can serve a life-saving purpose when discerned correctly, but it can also become a detriment when we allow it to consume us. This emotion is fear. For many of us, fear is a root that needs to be purged so we can freely move into surrender. It can be used as a mighty weapon to deter us from who we were created to be and it can manifest itself in many different ways. Many destructive behaviors can emerge from fear and we need to be on the defense against them. For example, worldly pride—also known as "conceit" or "vanity"—can be a byproduct of fear and gives way to self-sufficiency. It is driven by the need for acceptance and fear of rejection. If we fail to perform within certain parameters and expectations centered on the applause of man, then we fear a loss of approval. This motivation will deteriorate into an endless cycle of defining our worth by our human will to gain credibility in what the world values over what God values. That is a worthless pursuit. Jesus said, "And what do you benefit if you gain the whole world but are yourself lost or destroyed" (Luke 9:25, NLT).

I've watched this play out in the music industry more times than I care to count. It's heartbreaking. I recall a story about a very popular band that released a hit album right out of the gate. The music was intensely emotional and the deep, impacting lyrics carved into the depths of your soul. The message of each song was delivered with vocals and melodies drenched with conviction, pain, hurt, loss, and hope. The combination was entrancing.

At the time, a musician friend of mine was close with a member of that particular band who had decided to leave the group at the very onset and unfortunate peak of their popularity. He mentioned that the group was taking a serious detour from the foundation that had helped lead to their success. As they became "famous" in the eyes of the world, they completely disowned how they had originally come together as a worship band. They traded exaltation of the one true King for their own exaltation and they abandoned their profession of Christ because they feared the rejection of man. They lost the authentic identity they had when they started, and so did their music.

After a year or so, the group released their second album, which didn't climb the charts like the first did, and it was a continual decline. Now, years down the road, you don't hear much from them anymore, if at all. The world has gone silent in their favor, and now, sadly, so have they.

There is a natural bent for us to receive encouragement. Coming from the right people, it can validate our direction. However, when we idolize man's acceptance, we come in danger of losing ourselves and destroying what God has so graciously given. The applause of man provides a false sense of worth and out of a fear of losing that, we turn the other way because we don't want to lose what we've worked so hard to build. In reality, the monument erected for self is built on nothing but sinking sand (see Matt. 7:26–27). Pride driven by fear makes us stagnant and eventually fruitless.

It seems in today's culture, living in fear is a way of life. Just look around you and watch fear spread across souls from every race, religion, and culture. Take a look at the last two years up to the present. Lately it seems that we can turn on the news every day and expect to hear of a catastrophe, tragedy, or act of violence or terror. It doesn't seem "normal" nowadays without it. We have individuals who claim that it's the end of the world, trying to give precise dates (any questions about that, look up Matthew 24:36). Others are telling us to "stock up on guns and ammo" (that may just be a Texan thing), and to go buy land and build a bomb shelter.

Last year, we had one of the most active hurricane seasons on record, with storms that were relentless in their destruction. At the same time, wild fires raged in Oregon and Washington, earthquakes repeatedly struck Mexico causing severe damage and killing hundreds, and the Vegas strip became the site of the deadliest mass shooting in modern American history. Fearful circumstances continue to stack up one after the other. However, fear doesn't just rage on the outside in what we see—depending on the circumstances of life it also can rage inside of us spiritually, mentally, and emotionally, and be all-consuming, pushing us away from God's divine direction, guidance, and love. As followers of Jesus, we're given a different command, one of peace. Christ tells us, "Peace I leave with you; My peace I give to you; not as the world gives do I give to you. *Do not let your heart be troubled, nor let it be fearful*" (John 14:27).

My biggest problem on that river with my family was fear. I was crippled by it, and many of us, even as Christians, are living life that way. We ask: If I wholly surrender, what does that open my life up to? What kind of despair will I encounter? What will I lose?

We become fearful about taking a step toward God's instruction, fearful of where God has placed us, fearful of our past rising up to defeat us. We doubt, question, or defiantly ignore God's beckoning, then put on a face like we're just fine. We want others to believe we're surrendered, that we're the faithful few, and perhaps some of us are bold enough to think we're fooling God. But when the motives of our heart are revealed, we find our priorities are out of balance and confused. We find that we are cherishing false value and false credibility to choke out real joy, real hope, and real life. We're not surrendered to the ways of God but to the ways of man, and it is crippling us.

Jesus observed this kind of weakening fear among us in the days He walked the earth. He even confronted it in the story of the rich young ruler (see Luke 18:18–30) and He passionately encouraged us to move beyond such a stale and fruitless mind-set. Yet here we are, thousands of years later, still moving in that direction and operating with such defeat. We've found contentment with living life our way, even if there is a possibility of something better. These are our lives and we should be able to live them the way we want, we say. We don't see the need for accountability. We certainly don't want to "lose" anything. We believe that no one has the right to tell us what to do. And we don't believe we are hurting anyone. No harm, no foul, right?

Wrong.

Great harm is done when we're so self-absorbed. Our pursuits become nothing less than dark roads that lead to empty, decaying paths. When this happens, our self-indulgent pursuits allow evil to taint the blessing of God by encompassing us in the darkness of secrecy and defiance. We lose sight of godly pursuits as our focus moves inward to idolize me, myself, and I. A once vibrant heart dims with sorrow and despair, haunted by the choices we've made because we just want to do things our way. Then we try to push the darkness aside because we've got to show the world we're happy with our life, come what may. Even if we're a total mess, it's a mess we no doubt made on our own.

On the outside, we work hard to make it look clean and happy because our image is too important. However, on the inside, we're grieved and covered in shame as conviction radiates. Our souls are becoming a wasteland. In the most vulnerable moments, we know this to be true. But if anyone found out what we're really struggling with, if they found out the truth of our faults, we might lose acceptance. And without acceptance, who are we?

I've heard this defined at times as "the slippery slope." And unfortunately, it hits all of us at some point whether it's our own individual choices, or a family member or friend. I watched someone close to me begin this journey. They felt they needed to keep up an image and they compromised so much that they made choice after choice that would eventually cause heartache not only for them, but their family and friends as well. At first, much of it was done in secrecy but the more tangled in it they became, the more the reality of what was going on began to slip through the cracks.

No one could put a finger on exactly what was happening, but you could see a lifelessness begin to form in their eyes and an anxiousness grow in their spirit. The heaviness was apparent and the person many had known and loved began to fade as darkness took root. Their lifestyle choices—once set as a standard in order to preserve purity—began to change. They started to be more conscious of their appearance, which took center stage as their public image and perception became most important. They modified their behaviors and actions to fit a new mold of living as they abandoned righteousness and the demands of entitlement took over.

When it all came crashing down and the truth was uncovered, this person was devastated. I watched as anger took hold of them. Talks of "going away where no one can find me" were common at first, then attempted later, but they failed. They adopted hopelessness and any sense of peace they previously had was gone. All trust had been broken. A soul that had been dried up and become barren was desperately searching for new life and restoration.

When we truly surrender to God, the decision brings peace because we are chasing His righteousness. We trade in the self-entitlement that says, "I should be able to do whatever I want and I deserve it just because I'm breathing." It's replaced by a life full of God's love, purpose, favor, and clear direction as we live to be intentional and expectant followers of His divine footprints. That kind of living was our Creator's plan from the beginning of time and His plan will move from us into the generations that follow. Through a surrendered life, we'll confidently accomplish all that God created us to do and we'll leave a legacy of faithfulness when we depart this earth.

LOSE YOUR LIFE

In Matthew 10:39, Christ states a startling revelation: "He who has found his life will lose it, and he who has lost his life for My sake will find it."

Let's take an honest look at our lives as disciples. We're to die and give up our lives in order to live, not merely for our own selves, but for the sake of Christ and His mission. Our lives, built by our own self-sufficiency, must end to really begin. Seems simple, right? Maybe, maybe not. How are we to continue giving up our lives after the point of receiving salvation? How do we accomplish the standard set before us?

"And now, just as you accepted Christ Jesus as your Lord, you must continue to follow him. Let your roots grow down into him, and let your lives be built on him" (Col. 2:6–7, NLT).

When we become Christians, we're given a new life, one in which our sights must be set on the realities of heaven, not the things of the earth (see 3:1–3). Our aim is defined for us in Scripture: "In this new life . . . Christ is all that matters" (3:11, NLT).

As we move through life's stages of surrender, be encouraged to throw off the restraints of fear and a self-glorifying mentality. Be purposeful to follow the guide of Christ. By no means will this always be the "easy road." It's not going to be your five steps to success.

A while back when I was with a band touring with a solo artist, I remember meeting an absolutely unbelievable musician whose testimony blew me away. He had been running in some serious circles with stout connected instrumentalists. Because of this, he became very well-known and started getting gigs with some of the most prominent artists in the world at the time. These guys were the heavy acts and had the awards to prove it.

Around the time that his popularity was growing as a musician, he began to feel a call for ministry in the local church. He was at a crossroads. He did not feel he could continue to tour like he did and be planted to serve as he felt God was calling him to do. After much prayer and clarification, he made a decision to step away from the music scene and step into the local body of believers as a minister. To this day, he serves in the small church where he surrendered his life. He still receives calls every now and then to be a part of an incredible music act, but for the most part, he shows up every weekend and plays keys, which is not even his main instrument.

The neatest thing I noticed about him when we discussed his role in ministry was how content he was. He knew the calling God had placed on his life and he knew that where he had surrendered to serve was where he needed to be. Taking steps in that direction wasn't easy. His path ahead was going to be rocky. It was going to have its bumps and cause some bruises. The money, fame, and growing popularity were alluring. That's what most musicians dream of when they first start learning their new craft—and he had made it! He would even incur some loss, at least from a worldly standpoint. It was scary to think that he may never get to play at that level again. But he found contentment in the foundational truth that his aim was to please God above all others, especially himself.

The disciple's life is a journey. It's challenging and will be scary at times, but if we keep our focus on ourselves and our fear, we'll lose the authority of our witness and the strength of our joy. The victorious inspiration offered by Jesus puts an end to a self-gratifying life and plants the seed of a new one that is righteous in the sight of our heavenly Father. That life pleases Him and will bear fruit of eternal worth and significance. Surrendering to Christ is our first true act of worship as we abandon the life of worldly desire and find peace in the river of life where God has placed us. It's the first step and it's the only step that provides eternal freedom.

Going down the path of God's design is not always simple, and it may require you to leave all that the world deems necessary and important, but it's worth whatever comes your way. The world may scream at us to go in one direction and our Guide is calmly whispering to go in another. His lead might take us through serene, calm, and peaceful waters. Or sometimes, we may inexplicably end up in raging and terrifying white water. However, one destination has life and one destination will end in catastrophe. Thus, surrender is our starting point.

As we move forward, here are some questions to consider. Think and answer them truthfully. I also encourage you ask these questions to the trusted godly influencers and mentors in your life.

- Do you truly believe you're walking the path designed for your life?

- If the answer is "no," are you brave enough to ask why?

- Do you have anxious and worried thoughts regarding what surrender looks like in your life?

- What concerns may be holding you back?

- Could fear be hindering you from moving forward?

- What steps can you take right now that will begin to change the course of your life in surrender?

THREE

OBEDIENCE: BEAUTY IN WHAT WE CANNOT SEE

One theme that runs through Scripture like a steady river from beginning to end is obedience. Through the eyes of many biblical characters, we're given a front row seat to the positive and negative consequences of how one responds to God's commands. Obedience brings blessing, clear direction, and a hopeful future. Defiance brings harm and confusion—either in the present, future, or both. True surrender is all about obedience. Simply put, God's desire is for us to do what He asks.

Aboard the white-water raft, all the passengers had one solitary goal before them: Do what the guide tells us to do. I can tell you that when that objective became secondary, we were in jeopardy of failing to correctly navigate the course with strength and integrity, and ultimately, failing to finish with our lives intact. The same is true of us as disciples of Christ.

The phrase "obedience to God" seems rather broad. As Christians, we have a distinct authority God has given us: His word, the Bible. A fundamental step in obedience begins with following God's voice through the guidance of Scripture. For example, the most important commandment given, which details the very heart of surrender, is Matthew 22:37, NLT: "You must love the LORD your God with all your heart, all your soul, and all your mind."

In obeying this command, we're surrendering the totality of our being to the completeness of all of who God is and who He calls us to be. Following these guidelines in Scripture sets the foundation of being able to hear God's voice clearly and effectively in whatever He wants us to do. Then we can discern what paths we'll take that lead us to and through our calling and purpose. Finding joy in the course of our life is dependent on how clearly we can hear His direction and how intentionally we follow His lead. God's call to you may come in many different ways, and the key to success in God's eyes is in how we respond to that call. Do we ignore it? Do we say, "Hold on God. I've got something else going on." Or do we accept and step into that calling with trust and confidence?

Obedience may not always involve taking a huge step of faith into the unknown. Sometimes it can be as easy as smiling graciously at a passing stranger. If God places that desire on your heart, your smile might be the only uplifting display that individual sees all day. As God loves His creation, He may simply want to bring encouragement to that person.

There are also periods where obedience to a calling is hard and what's asked of us seems to make no sense whatsoever. We must remember that although we may see no light at the end of what seems to be a long, dark tunnel in our lives, God is actually leading us by the hand to an abundant garden of fruit at the other end.

THE BEAUTY OF THE BLIND

Have you ever been in a place so dark that you couldn't see your hand in front of your face? Truth be told, many of us can be pretty scared of the dark, especially here in the Western world where light is a privileged part of our equation for living. We need it and we rely on it. Everything's much clearer when we can see what's going on.

A few years ago, my in-laws took a trip to Africa. Although most of their stories seemed pretty surreal, there was one detail they mentioned that I could vividly imagine—the nights out on the plains. According to them, the night darkness was so dense you couldn't see anything. Now I don't know about you, but when I think about being out in the open African plains with lions freely roaming about in absolute darkness, I get nervous. I simply cannot imagine lying down to sleep and thinking to myself, *You know John, this could be your last night on planet Earth. If you had to get up and run, you don't even know where you'd go because you can't see! Awesome!*

What would be your plan of action if the unexpected occurred and some lion decided you were the perfect late night snack? That's not the best bedtime story to whisk me off to sleep. Curious how my in-laws responded, I asked what their train of thought was on nights like that. They said, "We trusted that where we were guided and planted for the night, we'd be protected."

The truth is, God sometimes calls us into the darkness to nourish our trust in Him. Although it can be frightening, it forces us to cling to Him for direction and give us a deeper understanding of His love. Let's begin with what is called "blind obedience," an act of faith that requires unsighted trust in a God who knows which way is best. A sense of destiny rises within us. We discern a call from God to move in a new direction. It may be unnerving or seem crazy. It may feel like a dead end, a bad decision in the wake of choices we have surrounding our lives. Friends and family may think what we're doing is absurd, yet we believe the direction has been confirmed.

So we take a step and begin the journey. The scene around us becomes dark; we either see a tunnel ahead or black as the darkest night. This kind of obedience involves coming to a cliff, looking over the edge, and thinking, "No way!" We feel around for some kind of assurance, but all we can hang onto is hope.

This kind of submission in heeding the call moves us into a delicate state of mind. Our emotions run high and the tension mounts. It can be easy to allow the feelings of fear, worry, and anxiety to overrun our spirits. It may be painful, difficult, and hard to understand, but the fruit on the other side of your long, dark tunnel of submission is beyond your realm of reality and it flows into God's glorious eternity. The work of God through us as His vessels doesn't remain earthbound. Treasures are being gathered in heaven as well (see Matt. 6:20).

When I first started college, I was going to take over the world as a drummer. Man, was I arrogant and prideful. I really think I believed I was one of the greatest things since sliced bread. The calling of being a full-time musician was apparent and had been confirmed in a plethora of ways. From godly counsel, biblical confirmation, encouragement from immediate family and friends, and a very generous financial gift for musical studies, the direction was clear. So I applied for college and became a percussion performance major.

I had an audition before the semester began to give the music professors and instructors a chance to see what I could offer as a freshman. I walked in thinking I was going to blow them away and walked out in utter disgrace. The audition was terrible. It's like I literally forgot how to play the drums.

Still, I managed to maintain my arrogance and kept my pride intact. The percussion professor quickly took note and made a statement to my parents that went something like this: "He's full of himself. He's got talent but he needs to be broken. I'm going to break him down and build him back up." My mom laughed and said, "Good luck." Turns out, he didn't need much luck. The river course began to change. Calm and serene waters were about to get really, really bumpy.

My first year ended with many bruises and some broken bones. Not only had I jumped out of the raft because of my own self-interest, but I didn't make my way back onto the raft until I slammed into some pretty serious rocks. To make matters worse, I got pulled under the pounding white water in a rapidly moving current called grades and college life. I was an ignorant and foolish idiot who, by the end of my freshman year, didn't know which way was up and which was down.

My parents made the decision to pull me from the out-of-state college I was attending to stay home a semester and enroll in a community college. Again, I found myself humiliated. They had just relocated to Houston, so any connections I had from where we previously lived were gone. Before college,

I was busy playing drums multiple days of the week and was fortunate enough to be making some money doing so. In Houston, I literally had no connection with anyone other than those I served in the local church where my father was an associate pastor. That was hard.

I had squandered what God so graciously provided. I didn't know what I was going to do. No community. No friendships. No connections. (You know . . . really good times. Not.) Praise the Lord for godly parents and godly counsel. They sat me down and encouraged me to pray and ask the Lord for His clear direction and guidance. At this point, they highly encouraged me to surrender. I had no choice. What else was I going to do? I'd been saved from drowning and now some reprogramming had to take place because I was a mess.

Spiritually, I didn't have a lot to offer. I was dry. I was in despair and I was angry. Nonetheless, I called out to God desperately and asked Him to lead me out of the pit I dug. I repented of my pride and raised the white flag to say, "Here I am." God's mercy straightened me up and gave me a fresh start. It took work, but it was worth it. He cleaned me up and put me back aboard the raft. Slowly, we pushed off from the shoreline and began our way down a new course.

After a few weeks of daily seeking out God's lead, doors began to open and new friendships began to form. New musical connections were also being made. During that semester away, great things started to happen and I got involved in musical opportunities that have led me to where I am today. I'm so thankful for God's gracious provisions.

After my grades improved at the community college and I developed my parents' trust again, I was allowed to return to the out-of-state college. By then, I'd become so busy playing drums with multiple bands and solo artists that it was hard to stay focused on school in the next semester. I was flying out almost every weekend to be involved with some gig or another. As the semester came to a close, it became evident that I'd need to make a choice: leave college and start a music career with some promise or stay in school and finish my degree.

That's a tough decision, one never to be taken lightly. I committed it to much prayer and sought out lots of counsel. I was scared of what the answer might be and it terrified me when the reality hit. It was time for me to step out and leave school.

Starting from my early years, society taught me that college is the only path to success. It's the only way we'll have a real chance to survive in this world. You want to make a good living, get a good education, and earn a degree. So naturally, my move was groundbreaking and scary. The darkness began to close in. The sun was setting and the river course ahead became black. I could hear the rush of waves surrounding and crashing on the rocks, but I couldn't see my hand in front of my face. I took a deep breath, gripped the paddle, and turned my ear to my Creator and Guide.

I wish I could say it became really easy. It did not. My extended family didn't understand. I was even called out and shamed greatly at a family gathering in front of everyone there. But inwardly, I knew this was the way God wanted me to go. So I started touring and playing gigs on the road. I was making money—not a ton—but I was able to make it work.

Those next few years were slim, but God was crafting and molding a path that would lead me to the purpose of His creation for me. After a few years passed, the Lord led me to yet another major decision that had to be made. It was time to step away from touring and find a more "stable" gig. I committed the decision to God and He made the way clear and did so quickly.

I had just gotten home from being out on the road and got a phone call from Second Baptist Church. They wanted to see if I'd consider being a musician for a Sunday night service there. I didn't know it then, but the opportunity would lead me to the stability I believed God had been calling me to and in ways I couldn't even imagine.

I took the gig, as it was then, but now it's so much more. After a few months, I was offered a position on staff at the church in the music ministry. After much prayer and godly counsel, I took it.

Since then, truly remarkable blessings have unfolded. A short time after coming on staff, I met the most beautiful lady in the world, Sarah, who soon became my wife. I proposed to her at Second Baptist in the sanctuary, which is where we were married a few months later. We now have two amazing children, and Sarah's a full-time mom. I'm an ordained pastor at the church and God has blessed me with opportunities musically that before were only far-off dreams. My family and I have been overwhelmed with God's gracious and abundant blessings. They're hard to explain in words. But they all come from to surrender and obedience.

A BIBLICAL EXAMPLE

Let's take a moment to look at Abraham, a man I place in The Blind Obedience Hall of Fame. For decades, Sarah and he had been earnestly praying for a son—the very son God had promised them. Even though both Abraham and Sarah were at an age that made having children seem impossible, God blessed them with the birth of their miracle child, Isaac. Years later, according to Genesis 22, the Lord instructed Abraham to sacrifice this promised one to Him as an offering.

> Now it came about after these things, that God tested Abraham, and said to him, "Abraham!" And he said, "Here I am." He said, "Take now your son, your only son, whom you love, Isaac, and go to the land of Moriah, and offer him there as a burnt offering on one of the mountains of which I will tell you." (Gen. 22:1–2)

Imagine Abraham's pain. He and Sarah desperately wanted a child and God made good on His promise to give them one by delivering Isaac to them. Now the boy was called to die by Abraham's own hands at the command of the Lord.

We're not given many more details about what occurred after Abraham received God's instruction, so I can only imagine what could have happened next. There could easily have been questions. Abraham may have questioned God. He may have even questioned himself and why He placed trust in a Being that would ask him to do something like that. The anguish and heaviness on his spirit were probably overwhelming. The promise made to him and Sarah would now be but a memory. They may have wondered, did we do something wrong? How could God ask us to do something that seems so inhumane?

Abraham's response is what inspires me. Genesis 22:3 tells us he got up early the next morning and moved forward with

God's directives. Then, in Genesis 22:9–18, God rewarded Abraham's obedience in His usual miraculous way.

> Then they came to the place of which God had told him; and Abraham built the altar there and arranged the wood, and bound his son Isaac and laid him on the altar, on top of the wood. Abraham stretched out his hand and took the knife to slay his son. But the angel of the LORD called to him from heaven and said, "Abraham, Abraham!" And he said, "Here I am." He said, "Do not stretch out your hand against the lad, and do nothing to him; for now I know that you fear God, since you have not withheld your son, your only son, from Me." Then Abraham raised his eyes and looked, and behold, behind him a ram caught in the thicket by his horns; and Abraham went and took the ram and offered him up for a burnt offering in the place of his son. Abraham called the name of that place The LORD Will Provide, as it is said to this day, "In the mount of the LORD it will be provided."

> Then the angel of the LORD called to Abraham a second time from heaven, and said, "By Myself I have sworn, declares the LORD, because you have done this thing and have not withheld your son, your only son, indeed I will greatly bless you, and I will greatly multiply your seed as the stars of the heavens and as the sand which is on the seashore; and your seed shall possess the gate of their

enemies. In your seed all the nations of the earth shall be blessed, because you have obeyed My voice."

As I read and reflect on that story, I keep thinking about how Abraham responded to God's calling. He didn't linger. He woke up and went early the next morning. He went at once. There was no delay in his obedience. He was confident in his trust in God. His trust was pure. He knew God—the infinite, sovereign Creator—could make a way beyond what Abraham could grasp in his finite human understanding.

In the story, we see that a great amount of trust had been established not only from Abraham to God, but from God to Abraham. God trusted Abraham enough to ask such a tremendous thing of him and, because of his obedience, God blessed Abraham immensely. He told him that his descendants would outnumber the stars and, through Abraham's offspring, all the nations on earth would be blessed "because you have obeyed me" (Gen. 22:18, NIV).

Abraham's personal relationship with God enabled him to clearly navigate the right path and make the right decision, despite what seemed to be dark circumstances. Through surrender, Abraham pushed past his limited human comprehension of a future promise and put his whole trust in the One who created both the promise and the child through whom the promise would be fulfilled. In turn, God unleashed an overwhelming blessing that we, in this lifetime, are still experiencing. If we are children of God through Christ by faith, we are Abraham's descendants included in the family blessing (see Gal. 3:6–9). Abraham's act of surrender catapulted that act of favor and assurance by God.

OBEDIENCE IS WORSHIP

Obedience is one of the most profound and important relational acts of worship. It's our response to God's governing in our lives as we say, "Here I am." Blind obedience brings us to the end of ourselves. We learn to trust that God will deliver the impossible and we must pray diligently for Him to follow through. Unfortunately, we often stop at this point. We hold up our hands and say, "Enough! I'll go to the ends of the earth, but not like that!"

What would have been the outcome if Abraham had reacted that way? Isaac could have been killed or taken away. God could have stripped Abraham of the promise and replaced him with someone else He could trust. We don't know for sure, but the unfolding of the promise would have taken a serious detour.

No one can see the future. We cannot see what tomorrow truly holds, but God can—and He has a way for us to get there. His plan for us has a destination, even though we may not clearly see it. We're to move toward it by His footsteps in front of us as He leads and guides us. Following His understanding is the only place we'll find delight, even in times of sorrow or when the road seems too difficult. Proverbs 3:5 instructs us to trust in the Lord with all of our heart and lean not on our own understanding. Proverbs 3:6 continues to comfort us in saying that as we acknowledge and submit to God in whatever we do, He will then make straight our path to lead us to our right purpose.

This should be the aim of every Christian. When we're actively living this out, we're making the greatest impact in our sphere of influence and we find contentment, come what may. Surrender begins with obedience.

REFINING OUR IMAGE

Blind obedience takes us through the refiner's fire, a process used by God to remove any impurities that exist in us so we can clearly reflect His divine image. It can often be misunderstood because it calls for endurance and perseverance through adversity, rejection, failure, loss, or any other afflictions we meet along the course of life.

> He will sit like a refiner of silver, burning away the dross. He will purify the Levites, refining them like gold and silver, so that they may once again offer acceptable sacrifices to the LORD. (Mal. 3:3, NLT)

Through such circumstances, God brings us to a point where our only option is to surrender because we have nowhere else to turn. Our sinful humanity limits us from solving the problem on our own. The struggle is too strong and water too rough to navigate without supernatural help.

It's easy to want to run in the other direction when we encounter the refiner's fire, but as a reminder, it's not something to turn away from. God is reshaping our will to align with His. This involves His discipline and correction, and can leave us feeling alone and in the dark. We can be left confused, confounded, wondering, "How did life end up here? I thought I was doing well!" Although these actions of the Lord's discipline can be uncomfortable, Proverbs 3:11 says we should never rebuke it: "My son, do not despise the LORD's discipline, / and do not resent his rebuke" (NIV).

Surrendering to God during these refining times creates a beautiful outcome because we can then live our lives in the purest pursuits of heaven, producing present and eternal fruits of righteousness. God's amazing love is put greatly on display toward us in these seasons. Hebrews 12:5–11 encourages us in this word:

> And you have forgotten the exhortation which is addressed to you as sons,
>
> "MY SON, DO NOT REGARD LIGHTLY THE DISCIPLINE OF THE LORD, / NOR FAINT WHEN YOU ARE REPROVED BY HIM; / FOR THOSE WHOM THE LORD LOVES HE DISCIPLINES, / AND HE SCOURGES EVERY SON WHOM HE RECEIVES."
>
> It is for discipline that you endure; God deals with you as with sons; for what son is there whom his father does not discipline? But if you are without discipline, of which all have become partakers, then you are illegitimate children and not sons. Furthermore, we had earthly fathers to discipline us, and we respected them; shall we not much rather be subject to the Father of spirits, and live? For they disciplined us for a short time as seemed best to them, but He disciplines us for our good, so that we may share His holiness. All discipline for the moment seems not to be joyful, but sorrowful; yet to those who have been trained by it, afterwards it yields the peaceful fruit of righteousness.

As we closely examine this passage, God is instructing us to embrace the love He's lavishly pouring on us. This can be tough because when this occurs, I personally try to convince myself that His love seems misguided. In my own self-absorbed state, I want to push away because I simply don't like the way He's handling things. I remind myself of a child, one who can't handle the authority of correction. Discipline means accountability and accountability means holding a standard. God's standard is perfection.

Obviously no one has the capability to be perfect, which is why we need a Savior. Jesus, the only perfect person to walk this earth as fully God and fully man, bore our sin. He took it upon Himself so that we may be justified before God the Father. When we surrender to Christ and accept Him as Lord of our lives, we become part of His family as dearly loved children (see Eph. 5:1). We're given a new life, spiritually speaking, so at that moment we become infants who need to grow up. In order for us to thrive in this new world—God's kingdom—we must endure discipline. We must grow to become mature.

The refiner's fire is intentional and with the right perspective, it becomes a great gift to us because when the time is over, we've grown wiser, stronger, bolder, and more confident in our faith. It strengthens our witness and leadership as an example to the world of unparalleled joy in the midst of hardship. We're able to endure in a way that astounds those "looking in" on our lives because of the Lord's discipline.

Contrary to some very popular teachings in this day and age, endurance does not come from our positive thinking or motivational perception. We're able to endure because we've been through the correction of fire, Christ being made known to men. Those aren't easy words to read, but sadly this passage is overlooked in today's Christian landscape. Instead, the truths presented in Scripture regarding the realities of life are virtually ignored. We've adopted the Western worldview that tells us to be happy all the time, live in a dream world of our desires, and don't be sad. Look up, because the skies are clear above the clouds! This isn't reality. It's a lie.

Everyone will experience some sort of rejection as they move through life. Everyone will experience loss. If you're a dreamer and visionary, you'll hear "it's impossible" at least once. If you like to take risks, you'll eventually find out that you are unable to hit the mark every single time. If you have a talent or a craft and want to improve, you'll eventually hit a learning curve that will take a considerable amount of effort to master. At some point, you'll probably want to give up and some people in your life will encourage you to do so.

Most of us will struggle with low self-esteem and the loss of worth. We will all make "superficial" friendships that won't stick. Some of us will have mentors who end up making poor life choices that greatly hurt or possibly destroy their families, sever friendships, and cause us despair. Every single person that walks this earth will have low points in their life. Somewhere along our river ride, the vast majority of us will slow down enough to realize our strength alone is really not enough, and we need help. Outwardly, this is hard to admit. Deep down, this truth is our glaring reality.

Getting past the clouds can bring clear skies, but other clouds are sure to come along. Such things cannot be ignored, but choosing to focus on "happy" all the time can cause us to miss the greatest blessings our heavenly Father offers. Through struggles and hardships, God reveals to us our weaknesses and impurities, and He refines us. Ecclesiastes 7:3 can be an encouragement to us as it says, "Sorrow is better than laughter, / for sadness has a refining influence on us" (NLT).

The refiner's fire helps us realize the foolishness of "self-sustainability" and shows us that God's strength is perfect in our weakest moments (see 2 Cor. 12:9). When we assume a mindset that values comfort over obedience, we ignore His path because we pursue a lifestyle that demeans the very essence of who God is in our life. Jesus makes this statement outright in John 16:33: "In this world you will have trouble. But take heart! I have overcome the world" (NIV).

This message isn't a popular one nowadays. It certainly doesn't send me running toward to the door shouting, "Hallelujah! Praise God!" Instead, it actually stresses me out and makes me want to run away screaming, "This is for the birds!" Godly authority and godly accountability can be very hard and challenging. Our will is literally being broken so that we surrender to His. Man, that's tough. But there's a deeper well we must plunge into and, when our impurities are removed, we can better understand the absolute purity of a God who cares for us in greater ways than we'll ever know.

A DEEPER KIND OF LOVE

At this point, you may be wondering, "How can such a loving God allow His children to go through so much adversity when we're doing what He asks of us?" As we walk down the dark corridors of blind obedience, we often question God's love for us because our understanding is so limited. We can't see every detail of life in the past, present, and future as He does. That's purposeful! He is the sovereign One, we are not. Unfortunately, we too often try to put Him in a little box as if He's some kind of all-powerful genie who's here for our benefit.

We so badly want to believe that a loving God wouldn't allow such hardship that we quickly forget this treasure: God is so holy that it took the death of His only Son to make us right. In fact, that same God could obliterate us from existence for our sins if He wanted. He did it once and saved a few with a massive boat called an ark. The penalty for the sins we commit now is death and there's no other way around that truth. God could permanently remove us, but He chooses not to because of the redemption He offers us through Jesus Christ. That's how loving our God is.

Make note: Not all acts of obedience will bring difficulty and trial. Some will bring joy and blessing into your life immediately. When Jesus tells us He came to make our joy complete, He meant it (see John 15:11). This is certainly true, but it only comes from following His lead and trusting Him as our Guide. When our choice to follow the Father creates some sort of struggle, it's happening for a reason and we'll never know what's on the other side until we move forward.

Abraham didn't know exactly what would occur when he took his faithful and obedient steps to do as God commanded. However, through knowledge, trust, confidence, and faith, he believed God's amazing love would provide more than what he was able to physically see. God's protection, providence, and purpose were established in the unseen. And, as Abraham moved forward in the rough water that lay ahead, his obedience to the guidance of God enabled the saving grace he and Isaac experienced, and the treasure of a blessing that's almost incomprehensible.

There's not one thing I've personally experienced—joy or pain—when hindsight didn't reveal a purpose for it. I remember in third grade, my father moved our family from the Dallas area to East Texas to start a church. It was his hometown, so he knew quite a few people and for a while, we felt very welcomed. However, as the years moved forward, things began to change. Those were tough years and very slim financially. God in His amazing provision saw to it that our needs were provided for, but we got by with very little.

When middle school rolled around for me and my brother was in high school, our friendships drastically declined. We were the "preacher's kids," but not how most people define them. We sincerely sought to stay out of trouble, so we were labeled "goody-goodies" and became distanced from the party/popular crowd. Unfortunately, in a small town where there wasn't much to do, you either hung out with that group or became alienated. So we didn't do much hangin' out with anyone. Our situation allowed my brother and me to grow very close. We became each other's best friend.

It was hard on my father and mother as well. It seemed my dad was ridiculed endlessly for the calling God placed on his life and the direction of the ministry of our church. Small town people also like to chatter. That bled into our school life, as well. It was rough for quite a few years on every individual in our family.

However, this is also when God began to plant in my heart a true love and drive for music. I bought my first drum set when I was sixteen. Since I did not do much socializing after school, other than soccer practice, I would come home and practice and play until dinner and then practice and play again after dinner. That's where I began to passionately pursue and gravitate towards my love for drumming and I had a lot of time to focus on the craft.

I credit those "lonely" dedications of time to why I have the privilege and honor to be involved with music as I am today. God was preparing me for the path ahead. My brother and I are still close, and have been through a considerable amount of circumstances where we have needed to stand by one another. Had it not been for those years in a small east Texas town, I'm not sure things would be as they are in the present. Through those years, God taught me a lot about people and ministry and how to recognize individuals who are strategically placed in your path to drain you and pull you away from your purpose. I learned a lot about life and how to stay true to your calling, even when it feels like everyone around you is against you.

Wherever you may be on your journey, it's helpful to know that God is not wasteful. What we experience through the circumstances we are being guided through serve as growth and fertilization. God's love for us is more than we'll ever realize in the here and now. God genuinely desires to give us direction because He knows the path we should be walking and He sees what's best. Sometimes when following His guidance, questions will rise and that's okay. Just make sure your final decision is leading you to follow His footsteps, not your own.

ESTABLISHED IN THE UNSEEN

Proverbs 16:3 tells us that we're to commit to the Lord, whatever we do, and that's what will bring success. I love the New American Standard Bible translation: "Commit your works to the LORD / And your plans will be established."

The verse ends with the word *established*. In Hebrew, that word is *kuwn*. It's a verb that means "to make firm, to be fixed and steadfast," and it signifies the action of setting something in place and making sure it lasts.[1] The promise made to Abraham is still in motion, even though he is no longer physically walking this earth. God used Abraham's obedience to establish a reality that will continue for all eternity. That's quite profound when you really take the time to think about it!

Blind obedience requires faith. To paraphrase Hebrews 11:1, faith is being sure of what we hope for and certain of what we cannot see. In the times of your life when you're staring at the waters that lie ahead and you're terrified, but you know God is telling you to get into the raft, you must grab a paddle, climb aboard, steady your feet in His grip, and open your ears to all He has to say. It's a must for you to accomplish what He's calling you to do, and the course ahead will cultivate surrender. As you move forward, you'll begin to experience the magnificent beauty of what God has prepared for you.

FOUR

OBEDIENCE: THERE WILL BE JOY

As we worked our way down the river, everyone was exuberant when we passed through an especially treacherous rapid or set of rapids without flipping over. Even our guide would laugh a hearty laugh which, to be honest, creeped me out. But still, everyone celebrated with joyous shouts and glee—especially me.

It wasn't until the end of the course that we were all able to see how important our obedience really was. Each individual played a distinct role by intentionally following the command of our guide. The purposeful respect and submission of each person unified the body of the raft, keeping everyone who was onboard alive with inspiration, enthusiasm, and hopeful expectation that we were all going to be okay. Even in the midst of what seemed to be certain disaster, a rest and peace occurred that brought about joy. The only one out of the loop was me! You know why? Because I refused to listen and obey.

Joy is a product of obedience, and a true understanding of what obedience really is helps us move toward it with gladness and a willing spirit. Charles Spurgeon once wrote, "Remember you cannot have a half of Christ. You cannot have Him as your Redeemer but not as your Ruler."[1]

In healthy parent-child relationships, children understand that their parents are there to help them succeed and get a better grasp on life. They appreciate the fact that, although they may not always love the guidance, they know they're in a safe place. They realize their parents have their best interests at heart, and long to see their children become everything God created them to be. Sure, they'll put up a fight sometimes. They're growing up and testing boundary lines, and that's normal. But when the "aha" moment comes, they see the reward of obedience.

Our spiritual growth is just the same. The Lord longs for us not to just experience joy in "happy" circumstances, but to know it no matter what circumstances may arise. He is the ruler of joy! Being in God's presence is being in the fullness of joy (see Ps. 16:11). He's the most radiant, joyful being that exists. It's part of who He is. Thus, He wants His joy be an integral part of our existence. As we surrender, intentional obedience is what miraculously ties the two worlds together and opens doors of opportunity, possibility, and astounding victory we'd never encounter otherwise.

I love the way Oswald Chambers, the early twentieth century evangelist and teacher, described joy:

> Joy is the great note all through the Bible. We have
> the notion of joy that arises from good spirits or
> good health, but the miracle of the joy of God has

nothing to do with a man's life or his circumstances or the condition he is in. Jesus does not come to a man and say "Cheer up." He plants within a man the miracle of the joy of God's own nature.[2]

GIDEON: GOD'S CHOSEN TO SAVE A NATION

One of the most inspiring scriptural accounts to illustrate both intentional obedience and joy fulfilled is the story of Gideon in Judges 6–8. His obedience led him from being the son of a farmer into a leader and warrior who saved a nation. For seven years, the Midianites continually defeated the Israelites, who had been sinful through disobedience. They had become accustomed to worshipping idols, causing them to be separated from God's protection.

This created great fear of the enemy and forced the Israelites into hiding for the sake of survival. They found their hiding places in the mountains. Their disobedience had brought them unnecessary hardships and taken them away from the resting place of God.

It was a very difficult time for the nation. In desperation, they cried to the Lord for help. Eventually, He came to their aid in a most unusual form: a farmer. That was surprising because Gideon was not someone society would count as a worthy soldier, much less a bold, conquering leader. Yet, as we've witnessed time and time again, God sees beyond perceptions.

One day, while threshing wheat secretly in a wine press so the Midianites would not attack him and take the crops that belonged to his family, Gideon was visited by the angel of the Lord who said, "The LORD is with you, O valiant warrior" (Judg. 6:12). This strong statement probably caught Gideon off guard. It seems he assumed that the angel of the LORD made an error in the use of a personal pronoun. Gideon's response seems to give way to gentle correction.

> Then Gideon said to him, "O my lord, if the LORD is with *us*, why then has all this happened to *us*? And where are all His miracles which our fathers told us about, saying, 'Did not the LORD bring us up from Egypt?' But now the Lord has abandoned us and given us into the hand of Midian." The LORD looked at him and said, "Go in this your strength and deliver Israel from the hand of Midian. Have I not sent you?" (6:13–14)

Note that this text points out that the Lord "looked at him." Another interpretation reads that the Lord "turned toward" Gideon.[3] This was done with purpose. It was a look of intentionality that said, "I mean business, Gideon." The call and command of our Creator is not one to take lightly. Then to focus the attention even more on Gideon's new role, the Lord essentially says, "No, Gideon. I'm not talking about 'us.' I'm talking about 'you.' I've sent you. You're the warrior. It is 'you' who will deliver Israel from the hand of the Midianites."

Gideon responds as most of us probably would: "O Lord, how shall I deliver Israel? Behold, my family is the least in Manasseh, and I am the youngest in my father's house" (6:15).

In today's cultural context, Gideon's reply might read something like this: "What? You've got to be kidding! There's *no way* that's going to happen. Did you really just say that? Do you know who you're talking to? I'm a *no one*. Capital 'N-O, O-N-E.' No one."

God, in His infinite wisdom, sovereignty, and understanding, doesn't give way to finite human reasoning here. His calling to Gideon isn't bound by human limitation and strength. He continues to guide Gideon through the waters of doubt and fear as He makes this statement: "But the LORD said to him, 'Surely I will be with you, and you shall defeat Midian as one man'" (Judg. 6:16).

God assures Gideon that he will defeat the Midianites before the battle even occurs. And He tells him it's actually going to be a lot easier than Gideon can even comprehend. God's strength in our weakness is untouchable. As a matter of fact, the writer of Hebrews refers precisely to that truth in regard to this event in history when he writes: "Their weakness was turned to strength. They became strong in battle and put whole armies to flight" (Heb. 11:34, NLT).

This lesson applies to every one of us. No matter how big or how small, no matter how simple or how absurd we might believe the steps to be, it doesn't matter. When God says "go," we must move and listen to our Guide as He navigates us through our course. Our inadequacies complement God's strength. When we stand in our most humbling circumstances and begin to take intentional strides toward Him—even though we feel we have nothing to offer—God shows us some truly awe-striking displays. He accomplishes great things. However, the usefulness of His strength through us can be deterred by our failure to do exactly as we're told.

Gideon still needed some confirmation, which is understandable. He asked for a sign and the angel of the Lord was gracious enough to provide it.

So Gideon said to Him, "If now I have found favor in Your sight, then show me a sign that it is You who speak with me. Please do not depart from here, until I come back to You, and bring out my offering and lay it before You." And He said, "I will remain until you return."

Then Gideon went in and prepared a young goat and unleavened bread from an ephah of flour; he put the meat in a basket and the broth in a pot, and brought them out to him under the oak and presented them. The angel of God said to him, "Take the meat and the unleavened bread and lay them on this rock, and pour out the broth." And he did so. Then the angel of the LORD put out the end of the staff that was in his hand and touched the meat and the unleavened bread; and fire sprang up from the rock and consumed the meat and the unleavened bread. Then the angel of the LORD vanished from his sight. When Gideon saw that he was the angel of the LORD, he said, "Alas, O Lord GOD! For now I have seen the angel of the LORD face to face." The LORD said to him, "Peace to you, do not fear; you shall not die." (Judg. 6:17–23)

Gideon now was ready to step aboard the raft and steady his position. The Lord had great plans to bring freedom to His people through Gideon; however, it required a delicate balance of decisions based on obedience. As the white water raged ahead, Gideon needed to tune in carefully to where the

Guide would lead, determining the success of man or the success of God. One would bring disaster. The other would bring life, rest, and peace.

REMOVING FALSE SECURITY

Apparently Gideon was riding on a fast-moving current because God didn't delay in the navigation.

> Now on the same night the Lord said to him, "Take your father's bull and a second bull seven years old, and pull down the altar of Baal which belongs to your father, and cut down the Asherah that is beside it; and build an altar to the LORD your God on the top of this stronghold in an orderly manner, and take a second bull and offer a burnt offering with the wood of the Asherah which you shall cut down." Then Gideon took ten men of his servants and did as the LORD had spoken to him; and because he was too afraid of his father's household and the men of the city to do it by day, he did it by night. (Judg. 6:25–27)

The first direct instruction given to Gideon was to remove false gods, images, and altars that were being used for idolatrous worship and replace them with an altar built to the one true God. This is vital for us to understand as well. Idols come in many shapes and forms and they can easily slither their way into a very prominent role in our lives. They become an object of worship, just like they did with the Israelites, and they turn our ear and gaze toward a voice that wants to destroy us rather than allow us to thrive. Give it long enough and that idol will eventually flip your raft and may even cause you to drown.

God was setting His rightful place as the true Guide of a nation so that His people could experience the purest freedom, which they would never be able to attain on their own. As you can clearly see, their way trapped them in a world of fear, anxiety, and worry. They failed to realize that God's righteousness brings peace (see Isa. 32:17).

Tearing down the altar of Baal did not seem to be an easy task, as it took two bulls and ten men. The directive also made Gideon fearful, so much so that he took care of the matter at night. Not only did he fear the "men of the city," in this culture the worship of these gods was taken very seriously and such an offense was punishable by death (see Judg. 6:30). He was also fearful of his "father's household."

We see God draw a very distinct line in the sand with this request. His holiness and honor are above those of our earthly family, especially if the members of our family have opened their hearts in worship to demonic beings and pursuits of evil idolatry or have engrossed themselves in sin.

We must be willing to obey God, even if it means creating a division within our family. Christ confirms this in Luke 14:26 when he says, "If anyone comes to Me, and does not hate his own father and mother and wife and children and brothers and sisters, yes, and even his own life, he cannot be My disciple."

(Please note: These words can be easily misunderstood. I have known men who have sacrificed their families based on what they would say was the "call of God." There can be a sad reality that exists in many ministers' homes—broken families.

They are divided because the father or mother, or both gave all their time to a "mission.")

When God entrusts a family to you, they should immediately become your first priority. Your family is your first mission field, a husband to his wife or wife to her husband and then to their children. Take serious caution in this. When married and an opportunity is presented, the "two who have become one" must seek God fervently in prayer before a move is made. Ask the Lord for considerable confirmation. If God wants you to go, He will make sure you get the message.

There may arise a time in which you may not see eye to eye with your spouse. At that point, it becomes the responsibility of the husband to make the decision he feels God has set before the family. The wife must then be wise and submit to the spiritual leadership of her husband. Men, this is a very serious role the Lord has placed on us. Be careful not to sacrifice your family on the altar of "self" so that your self-worth may be promoted. Too many families have been dismantled because of this one thing. The statement "This is what God is telling me we should do" is too severe to throw around. To use such a phrase for our own indulgence is foolish and ignorant, and one we will pay for later if our decision is not truly based on God's direction.

ALIGNING OUR HEARTS

When it comes to parental relationships, we're called to honor our father and mother. This is the first commandment with a promise (see Exod. 20:12). However, our heart must first be aligned with God's heart. Before the commandment to honor your father and mother is laid forth, the first three commandments in Exodus 20:3–5 explain how we're to worship God and keep far away from worshipping idols.

Here in the story of Gideon, we see this take place. It's a clear picture that God's commandments are far more important and vital than those of any earthly family in godless pursuits. Our relationship to God and His righteousness are first and we're to be obedient to that call. As we listen and follow His lead down the river of life, God will prepare the hearts of those who will need to follow, no matter what lies ahead.

> So the Spirit of the LORD came upon Gideon; and he blew a trumpet, and the Abiezrites were called together to follow him. He sent messengers throughout Manasseh, and they also were called together to follow him; and he sent messengers to Asher, Zebulun, and Naphtali, and they came up to meet them. (Judg. 6:34–35)

Gideon, although tentative, had faith enough to do what God asked of him. Through his faithfulness and obedience, God began to assemble a group of men who would overthrow a vast army and begin to restore freedom and peace for a people imprisoned from a desire to do things their own way, following the pattern of the world.

When Israel muddied the waters and allowed false gods into their lives, they placed their hope in a deceptive sense of security. They sought to serve the one true God as well as the gods of man. Such pursuits weakened their foundation and set them toward treacherous waters, from which they were unable to escape on their own. In order to set things straight, God's holiness had to reign and be restored among their hearts through worship to Him and Him only.

PURGING IDOLS

The worship of any idol exchanges light for darkness. It removes the completeness of God's protection over us. Idolatrous worship is a serious matter to a Holy God who calls us to be single-minded in our devotion to Him.

> Who may climb the mountain of the LORD?
>> Who may stand in his holy place?
> Only those whose hands and hearts are pure,
>> who do not worship idols
>> and never tell lies.
> They will receive the LORD's blessing
>> and have a right relationship with God their
>> savior.
>
> (Ps. 24:3–5, NLT)

This is well-illustrated for us in the story of Gideon. As the Israelites engaged in the idolatrous community of the world, they jeopardized a right relationship with God, removing blessings and peace, and opening themselves up to judgment. In the Ten Commandments, God gave the decree that idol worship was off limits. The Israelites didn't want to listen, so God lifted His protection from them because of their disobedience. He allowed continual defeat and a fearful unrest to stir within the people. That unrest can exist within us today due to idols in our own lives. Complete surrender requires the removal of false security offered by false gods and idols. It removes darkness from our lives and allows us to be fully aware of God's direction, and wholly available and obedient to Him. We must destroy idols in our lives. Acknowledgment is the first step, then repentance.

But what is considered an idol? Pastor and author Tim Keller defines an idol as this: "When anything in life is an absolute requirement for your happiness and self-worth, it is essentially an 'idol,' something you are actually worshiping."[4]

Idols come in many different forms and can be characterized by many different attributes. Idols will cause us to compromise values and priorities so we don't have to let go of what we feel is so precious, so right, so relatable, or so relational. We can often use them to our advantage and are even willing to bargain purity for pleasure.

In other ways, we'll use these idols to attain a status of importance and dominance in the workplace, at school, or at home. They become such an obsessive trait that we simply don't want to separate ourselves from them. Interesting to note, at one time we may have felt convicted to remove these idols; but now, since we've pushed that conviction to the side enough times, our sensitivity has been dulled.

In my life, I've had quite a few struggles in this area and really had to do some personal introspection to figure out the motives behind my madness. I used to believe that people's perception of you is what defined you, and that what you did behind closed doors really wasn't all that important. Then I discovered that what is done in secret will eventually be brought to the light. My image was an idol. That kind of idol can come in many different forms.

I've never been one to focus on clothing and what I wear or what name is on the tag. I've not been concerned with what kind of shoes I have on my feet or how fit my suit is. That's not ever really been my thing. Now, because of that, I have family who actually is concerned because they've seen me wear the same clothes seven years in a row and never buy a new shirt. So they've made up their minds that they'll just get me clothes from time to time.

My "image idol," if you will, was about importance. How "important" did people think I was? How "established" was I to those who knew me and those who first met me? I really liked to talk about myself and I really enjoyed the look on people's faces as I elaborated on what I did and who I knew. I feel sorry for those who met me early on and commend those who are still my friends because a simple handshake was like a button one would push as an immediate download of information. I began to do this enough to where my sensitivity to my running mouth didn't register and I became "that guy" at social events. But to me, how I was perceived is who I was, and that belief is far from the truth.

If we really want to be effective influencers to those around us, authenticity is key. If we're not genuine, the truth of who we really are will be revealed in time. Who I was in public was far more valuable to me than who I was in private, and I hid it very, very well. The Lord's discipline works in the opposite rhythm of our sin. When I was dishonest in public, the truth would be revealed in public. The motive of my heart was impure and God weighs our motives. Proverbs 16:2 says, "People may be pure in their own eyes, / but the LORD examines their motives" (NLT).

My motives were all about me, myself, and I. I had raised an unseen statue to my self-worth. My idolatry was deteriorating and weakening my character and my integrity as a follower of Christ. I had to have the perception of importance in order to be happy.

Take some time to think about this. Is there anything in your life right now that you feel you must have in order to be happy, something that you really believe makes you look and feel important? This is not an exhaustive list by any means, but it's a starting point to see the idols that may be standing in your life right now.

- A better looking car: *I gotta get something with a certain brand name that holds high value in the eyes of others.*

- A bigger house: *I can't have the smallest house on the block or the smallest home among my friends.*

- The perfect physique: *I'm gonna obsess over food and make sure I hit the gym everyday so I can look just like that "airbrushed to perfection" personality on that magazine that doesn't paint a picture of reality.*

- Designer clothes: *I can't go out and buy something from that discount store. I must buy that $250 sweater because someone might stand close enough to me to see the tag buried behind the collar.*

- Sports: *My son/daughter can only be involved with the best. It doesn't matter what we need to sacrifice or what kind of lifestyle they learn. They'll work that out later. It's too embarrassing otherwise.*

- A better job: *I can't work in this environment. I'm too blocked in, or I'm just too strong of a leader to be led by someone like that.* (Side note here: You'll never reach the full potential of the vision God has in store for you until you can effectively serve someone else's vision.)

- Music: *I've got to be relatable to my peers and coworkers, so I'll listen to the music they listen to, which degrades women, talks about taking drugs like its cotton candy, and encourages me to do some unbelievably unhealthy things to my body and my spiritual and emotional well-being.* (Another side note: As a musician, I can tell you that music is dangerous ground. There are many songs we can get wrapped up in and not realize the message that's being poured into our minds. We get carried away by a beat or memorable melody within the song and, without knowing it, feed our spiritual mind with things that if we were to hear them without the instruments going on in the background, we'd be appalled. Listen to what you're feeding yourself. Don't be ignorant of the message.)

- Social Media: Okay guys—I'm just gonna level here. Social media as an idol is a problem for many of us on a personal level. And though we may be willing to admit it, several of us are unwilling to take any action to be diligent in securing boundaries. If you are unable to take a full break from any kind of social media outlet for just one or even two days, you need to be honest with yourself and admit there might be an issue. Don't just acknowledge it and do nothing. Create intentional boundaries.

We've got to tear these idols down and replace them with worship aimed to please our Creator and Guide. He cares deeply about our pursuit of purity. We are His workmanship and a representation of Jesus Christ. That demands our respect, from what we allow into our minds and hearts to what comes out of our mouths, from the actions we take to the priorities we place to the relationships we build.

Will we fall short? Absolutely. Is there grace for when we do? Yes. But this doesn't give us the freedom to just do what we want, when we want, how we want (see Rom. 6:1–2). That's a very selfish way of thinking and living.

As you'll recall, I wrote a story in chapter 2 of someone close in my life who ventured down a "slippery slope" in the pursuit of "my way or the highway." They began to deeply value the acceptance of man over the acceptance of God. Their heart had become darkened with the idol of entitlement, the idol of image, and the idol of man's approval. Thus they made detrimental life choices caused by a false belief system that had become a sinking foundation.

But the story didn't end there. Once the truth was uncovered and wrongful actions were acknowledged, God abundantly provisioned His grace and this individual started the hard and victorious work of restoration through repentance, cutting away idols that were dealing them death. Through surrender and obedience to God's direction over their own way, they rebuilt and reconstructed their lives and the lives of those who had been so devastated by this person's sinful choices.

Trust has been renewed. A new freedom has been established. Shame, guilt, and condemnation have no hold—those chains have been cut away. The power of God has been revealed and a new understanding of surrender has taken place as the old life is gone and a new, vibrant life glows brighter than ever before.

You might be wondering why you feel held back and disconnected from what God is calling you to do. You may be wondering why you feel so numb to it all. This could very well be the cause. Idols and impurities that exist within our lives create a distance and separate us from the purity of God, causing us to miss His guide in the waters ahead. They value and feed on the acceptance of man. Though they may cause one to feel embraced, respected, and loved, those feelings are a mask of light that hide a darkness so vile it corrodes the soul, a poison that creates decay. But praise be to God that we have hope and it comes through acknowledgment and repentance, which will provision restoration.

I encourage you to ask the Lord to reveal the impurities or idols that exist in your life. As they're exposed, recognize them, tear them down, and remove them so that you exalt the only One who is to be praised by the purest offering of your life. This opens the door to a surrendered heart. We must not allow anything to take the place of loving God with all our heart, soul, and mind (see Matt. 22:37).

These are not dogmatic principles set in place to hinder us. They actually protect us and protect our witness. God's word set the standard; thus, we have a mandate to reach for the highest levels of purity in our everyday living so we may be holy vessels. We're to be *in* the world, not *of* the world. When the Israelites participated in idol worship, it led to their impurity and ultimately their destruction. But Gideon's obedience to follow the Lord's instruction redeemed Israel. This is part of surrender—and truthfully, our Savior deserves nothing less.

GOD'S REALITY VS. HUMAN IMPOSSIBILITY

After the idols have been removed and a right spirit is restored within us, it's our responsibility to start walking in the way of God's direction. This can prove to be challenging, especially when we're not able to make sense of the Lord's directives. But God's reality extends far beyond our impossibilities and, when we give way to full devotion in surrender and tune in to our Guide, the raging water before us becomes a course we're able to effectively navigate.

Gideon watched this take place right before his very eyes. He must have swelled with pride as those 32,000 people gathered to fight, standing with him against the enemy. Then, in Judges 7:2–3, God proceeds to burst Gideon's proverbial bubble.

> The LORD said to Gideon, "The people who are with you are too many for Me to give Midian into their hands, for Israel would become boastful, saying, 'My own power has delivered me.' Now therefore come, proclaim in the hearing of the people, saying, 'Whoever is afraid and trembling, let him return and depart from Mount Gilead.'" So 22,000 people returned, but 10,000 remained.

Just imagine how Gideon felt as he probably stood there with his shoulders slumped and his mouth dropped down to his chest, watching more than half of his army run away in fear. Talk about another "freak-out" moment!

As a new leader of men, Gideon probably didn't want to show much anxiety, even though he really was about to lose it. However, God wasn't done.

Then the LORD said to Gideon, "The people are still too many; bring them down to the water and I will test them for you there. Therefore it shall be that he of whom I say to you, 'This one shall go with you,' he shall go with you; but every one of whom I say to you, 'This one shall not go with you,' he shall not go." So he brought the people down to the water. And the LORD said to Gideon, "You shall separate everyone who laps the water with his tongue as a dog laps, as well as everyone who kneels to drink." Now the number of those who lapped, putting their hand to their mouth, was 300 men; but all the rest of the people kneeled to drink water. The LORD said to Gideon, "I will deliver you with the 300 men who lapped and will give the Midianites into your hands; so let all the other people go, each man to his home." (Judg. 7:4–7)

Poor Gideon. I cannot fully grasp the stress he probably felt in that moment. Do you think there were many self-help books around in that day? Probably not. But if there were, Gideon might have started to recite something of like this: "Okay, based on the papyrus reading from this morning, what I need to do is count to ten; then, take three deep breaths as I count back down to one. Do this seven times and . . . then . . . forget it. I'm just going to start screaming. Wait—no. Due to the lump in my throat, I think I'm just going to cry."

And just like that, the mighty army of Israel went from 32,000 to three hundred. Good grief! That's just crazy. But as it turns out, only three hundred men were needed to ensure defeat. When God's provisions are at work, that's really all we need because He's already sealed our victory. That's part of the joy of following Him. He's going to carry out His plan and what He asks you to do no matter the odds because the odds are not even negotiable. The Lord's sovereignty makes sure of that. Where the Lord guides, He provides.

IT'S YOURS FOR THE TAKING

As illustrated in the story of Gideon, God doesn't call us into something we're ill-equipped to do so we can miserably fail. His success goes in our favor as we intentionally seek His perfect will. The amazing truth is that His grace covers us before we even take our first step.

> Now the same night it came about that the Lord said to him, "Arise, go down against the camp, for I have given it into your hands. But if you are afraid to go down, go with Purah your servant down to the camp, and you will hear what they say; and afterward your hands will be strengthened that you may go down against the camp." (Judg. 7:9–11)

God is in full control of our seemingly insurmountable situations, just as He was for Gideon. Once we're aware of this, we have nothing to fear and nothing to worry about. What a gift! That treasure brings joy as a constantly flowing river to revive us when we feel alone and defeated.

It's understandable that in the moment, everything can be blurry and these certainties can be hard to remember. That's just fine. Just know that the Lord has already equipped you with a Purah to support you when you feel faint. This is precisely why it's so important to be wise with our friendships. We need friends who will speak God's truth into our lives, bless us with hope in despair, keep us accountable to our calling, and pray for us on our journey. This is especially true when we walk into something that's a greater challenge than we anticipated at first, which isn't uncommon when we're in enemy territory.

Although God's path often isn't the one of least resistance, remember He doesn't bring confusion. God provided Purah to be a witness to what He was doing, which probably helped relieve Gideon of confusion in times when he was uncertain. Just because you meet criticism and even cynicism while taking the submissive steps doesn't mean you're out of God's will. Even though there may be fear and anxiety in the steps you're taking, it doesn't mean God isn't with you, and that you've made a grave mistake. Many times, God uses such seemingly hostile environments to prune and purify your journey. As we discussed in the previous chapter, opposition is often part of the refiner's fire, so be mindful of any unhealthy fear creeping alongside you.

There is a difference between healthy fear and unhealthy fear. One allows you to remain peaceful and keeps you moving forward. The other paralyzes, steals joy, and causes confusion and panic. Healthy fear brings you closer to God; unhealthy fear drives you away from God. It comes down to trust. Are you God-dependent like Gideon or self-sufficient? Remember, if God supplied the command, then the prize is yours for the taking.

VICTORY

Obedience facilitates victory, not defeat. There's no greater joy than victory, especially when everyone around you says it's impossible and the circumstances scream, "Get out while you can!" When we finished the white-water course, it was one of the happiest moments of my life. It was quite a profound moment standing on the shoreline, looking back at the river I really believed would claim my life. Our guide was satisfied, as well. I even got a tap on my shoulder and a "Good job, man. Didn't think you were gonna make it. But you did."

When we're sure of the call, the victory is waiting, despite what surrounds us—even when it feels like we're in enemy territory. Scattering our foes is one of God's unique specialties. That's why His word in Romans 12:19 tells us, "VENGEANCE IS MINE, I WILL REPAY."

As we continue with Gideon's story, God shows us just how powerful His movement can be.

> When they blew 300 trumpets, the LORD set the sword of one against another even throughout the whole army; and the army fled as far as Beth-shittah toward Zererah, as far as the edge of Abel-meholah, by Tabbath....
>
> They captured the two leaders of Midian, Oreb and Zeeb, and they killed Oreb at the rock of Oreb, and they killed Zeeb at the wine press of Zeeb, while they pursued Midian; and they brought the heads of Oreb and Zeeb to Gideon across the Jordan. (Judg. 7:22, 25)

The Midianites didn't stand a chance, even though their number was as numerous as a swarm of locusts and they owned more camels than they could count (see 7:12).

The Lord took three hundred men and defeated a powerful enemy like it was a walk in the park. Without Gideon's faithful obedience, this event would have been recorded differently. This shows that from start to finish we must stay the course and not jump out of the raft when uncertainty arises. A beautiful outcome is waiting, but this can only happen when we remain obedient to what God tells us to do. Otherwise, when we disobey, we become stubborn and fearful, limiting the full capacity of God's work and missing great victories.

JOY

The account of Gideon shows us that obedience, even when seemingly absurd, brings great victory, restores honor, and upholds our character. When you realize the Lord is with you in the midst of battling the raging currents of the course He's called you into, you'll find a peace so great that it will astound—even confuse—the wisest of the world. Our joy becomes complete when we realize our Creator is trying to get our attention so that, through faithful obedience, we can abundantly live the life He has for us and accomplish great feats by Him and for Him. The way is already prepared, but our faithfulness to His details determines our destiny.

FIVE

THE BREAKING POINT

Racing down the Ocoee River, I wasn't prepared to hear these words from our guide:

"Okay, everyone listen to me very carefully! We're coming up on a Class V rapid called the 'Can Opener.' We have to go right through two boulders. If we hit either boulder to the right or left, our raft will split in two!"

What? Seriously? That's it. On that fact alone, we're doomed!

Once again, I found myself frozen in distress. Funny how fear raises its ugly head when we venture into the unknown. As I looked onward with a nervous gaze, I was pretty certain I was going to pass out from fear of the terrifying sight that was staring back at me. Massive, towering boulders jutted out of the water with the most jagged edges I'd ever seen. I thought for sure our raft would be split in two as we smashed into those deadly boulders at a downright scary speed.

Lights out! I thought. *We're all about to meet our Maker!*

Then you know what I did? I just started screaming. Those screams turned into more of a screech as we approached the turbulent rapids ahead.

There I was, twelve years old, learning to be a man, girls regularly on my mind, and I was literally screaming at the top of my lungs because I was so scared. I'm pretty positive that kind of reaction doesn't win many points with the female gender. Not to mention, our guide was trying to tell us what we needed to do, but no one could hear him because I had gone ultrasonic on the raft. I had reached the breaking point.

There are circumstances that will come up in which our own class V can openers will emerge and nearly defeat us just by the sight of them. We'll have troubling, unseen circumstances that can cause great danger if we're not being watchful. Without proper instruction and obedience, these issues will haunt and hover over us. So that's when we've got to ask: Who are we listening to? On whom does our faith rest? Who are we relying on to help us? To rescue us? To guide and lead us so we'll get through what seems to be insurmountable obstacles? And one more very important question: Can we even hear our Guide when these times come around?

The roughest rapids of life range in their intent and purpose. They can be tests provided by God, consequences of our sin (sometimes they can be a mix of both), or they can also simply be tough circumstances brought about just by living life. Whatever they may be, both purging and pruning are involved. It's important to remember that what may seem to be massive obstacles can actually help us define our identity as Christ followers. These life "can openers" pry us open and begin the process of removing any sort of self-reliance and self-sufficiency that remains. They'll call our bluff if we try to go through them alone, and the Enemy will try to use them to devour us, as Peter so plainly states in First Peter 5:8, "Be of sober spirit, be on the alert. Your adversary, the devil, prowls around like a roaring lion, seeking someone to devour."

These obstacles can range from the loss of a job, marriage problems, financial stress, broken trust in a once reliable friend, tragic loss of a loved one, seeking freedom from depression, anxiety, rage, and addictions. The list could go on and on. We're born broken and we live in a broken world. When we become believers in Christ, He mends that brokenness but the Enemy works hard to manipulate us into thinking we're still damaged. It can be a defeating cycle and the Enemy will use fear to try and control us, so all we hear is the raging water and roar of the waves that smash against the rocks, creating a diversion from the voice of our Guide, who calls out to us to help us and lead us through such difficult circumstances.

It's here in these moments that silencing ourselves within will allow us to hear His instruction and tune in to His voice, which is saying, "Stop. Don't let fear have its way. Quiet your thoughts, quiet your spirit, and listen. I am going to get you through this." If we pay close attention to our Guide, we will survive. Maybe not without a few bumps and bruises, but we'll make it. However, this victory will happen only by listening and cultivating our relationship with Christ, drawing near to Him and asking Him to draw near to us. Learning to be still, quiet, and patient when there seems to be disorder and likely catastrophe all around is a profound discipline, but it's worth the time.

THE COMMAND TO BE STILL AND SILENT

Silence is tough in a world crammed with technology that allows us to constantly be on the move. We engage in waves of activity as if the world will come to an end if we stop moving. We act as if the earth stays in rotation because we're constantly walking its surface. Silence is seen as a distraction, not a tool used for victory. As fallen creatures, we just don't seem to know when to stop and release the reins.

As we headed toward the terrifying white water, our guide knew exactly what to do to ensure the safety of everyone on the raft. So he called out: "Paddles up! Bring them in! We'll go right through—I'll direct from the back. Pull paddles in . . . now!"

At this point, he was letting us know that he was in total control and, as we listened intently to his commands, our response was to rest and let him take us through. At the greatest point of tension, we were told to stop fighting for our survival and allow our guide to lead us. After all, he knew the river so well and he identified with our fear and concern. However, he was the one capable of getting us through, not us.

God does the same. In multiple Psalms, we read of honest cries and pleas of the need of "rescue." And we also read of shouts of joy because of God's great "rescue."

> But I trust in your unfailing love.
> I will rejoice because you have rescued me.
> (Psalm 13:5, NLT)

Show me your unfailing love in wonderful ways.
  By your mighty power you rescue
  those who seek refuge from their enemies.
(Psalm 17:7, NLT)

Rescue me from the wicked with your sword!
(17:13, NLT)

He reached down from heaven and rescued me;
  he drew me out of deep waters.
(18:16, NLT)

Protect me! Rescue my life from them!
  Do not let me be disgraced, for in you I take
  refuge.
(25:20, NLT)

God loves to rescue His children, and He loves to draw us out of deep waters. He shows a grace that's beyond comprehension, especially when we've gotten ourselves into a mess. And wouldn't you know it? In total contrast to the things of God, the Enemy loves—and I mean loves—to come down on us, shame us, hover over us, tell us how much of a mess we've made. Condemnation is one of his specialties. It's so hard for us not to listen to the rapid spew of blame we sense all over us. Does this sound familiar?

"You got yourself in this mess, you gotta get out."
"Wow. Come on. Can't you get it right?"
"This is going to follow you for the rest of your life."

"You might as well give in; you won't ever be able break free from this."

"It's just too much for you to handle. The only way out is to end it. Free yourself."

The more we listen to the accusations involving shame and guilt, the bigger the boulders get, and it becomes easy to shy back and retreat into other harmful behaviors that isolate us and make us feel all alone. God calls to us in victory but all we choose to hear is defeat.

Do you know how hard it was to stop paddling and just sit as we rapidly sped between those rocks? As we approached the jagged stalwarts, my instinct to fight in order to make sure I survived kicked in. So in complete defiance of what the guide told us to do, I stuck my paddle in the water just as we were about to pass by the boulders. Well, that was stupid. As I dug in, I hit a small rock and, with great force, I was jolted into the air! Thankfully, my brother reached up and grabbed my knees and pulled me back to safety.

If only I'd done as I was told, that scenario would have never played out. But I didn't and I ended up paying a price, one that could have easily cost me my life. I was not still, I was not quiet, and I was not patient. I tried to handle the situation on my own. I thought I had the better solution despite the fact that the guide had trekked this river course before and knew exactly what needed to happen.

Psalm 37:7 says, "Be still before the Lord / and wait patiently for him" (NIV).

The instruction is twofold—to wait and wait patiently. When it seems we're about to run headfirst into unwavering boulders that could easily cause a great divide in our life, this principle should be our first pursuit of surrender. But when survival is at the top of the list, we start to fight and find that we're unwilling to wait, pray, and bring in our paddles to stop forcing our way through. For most of us, it can be difficult to stop and be still, so we become frantic and frail rather than silent and strong.

GOD'S PRESENCE WHEN HE SEEMS SILENT

My wife and I have been given a wonderful treasure in our children. When our first was born, as new parents we were just hanging on for dear life trying to figure it all out. In the first few months, we worked overtime to bring some comfort to our daughter after the traumatic stress of birth. Yes, it's stressful on babies too!

Newborn babies need lots of sleep, so when nap or bedtime came we would rock, bounce, swing, or whatever we found would work so that when she slept, we could sleep. Most of the time, this brought great comfort to her—a comfort we were more than willing to provide—and she'd sleep soundly. However, there did come a time when we had to teach her to fall asleep without our help. This wasn't just for us. She had to learn this very important life skill.

As you would expect, she immediately began to cry when we put her in her crib. The daily bedtime routine that brought comfort and refuge was gone. The new practice would be for her good, but it was hard for her to understand.

While working through this one evening, I placed her in the crib, stepped back, and stood in the doorway. She wasn't able to see me but I wasn't far away, just in case she needed me to pick her up for some reassurance. I stood in silence and listened to her cry (one of the hardest things to do as a new dad!). Immediately, the Lord began to flood my mind with truths pertaining to my relationship with Him as a child of Christ.

Here's the profound lesson I learned that day: Sometimes God has to take us out of our comfort zone to a place we feel would cause us great distress and fear. Because of that fear, we believe we'll be left alone, our needs abandoned, so we cry and scream. Though we don't sense Him, He's still with us. It then becomes vital for us to understand that, in these times, He may seem distant. But He is inviting us to sense His presence in a way we've never known before. We can find it when we become still and quiet, knowing that God will never leave us nor abandon us, even when He seems to be silent. Hebrews 13:5 encourages us in this word: "For God has said, 'I will never fail you. / I will never abandon you'" (NLT).

He's still directing our path down the river, still in total control. But we must be willing to release the comfort of feeling like we're in control so He can navigate us through the difficult circumstances that stand before us. There will be periods, by His great compassion and love, when God allows us to stay in a place of comfort for a season, a place where we're able to see Him, sense Him, and know Him deeply. This is critical for our growth. But He also knows we can't stay there forever because we have to move forward. It's too important for the purpose for which you and I were created. God allows those seasons for encouragement. But to accomplish the purposes He created us to be a part of, He shakes away those comforts to awaken in us a deeper understanding of His presence and care in the realm of what appears to be His silence.

We can trust He is still there. We can hold on to what we know is true, even when we feel He has removed us from His arms. This is very hard at times, but He's getting us to our breaking point. God is still near, there to protect us if danger does arise, but He longs for us to understand peace when we feel He is distant as well as the times when He is purposefully making His presence known. When the breaking points stand ahead and we're bracing for impact, instead of screaming because things aren't going the way we think they should, our initial response should be stillness. This is when God can easily draw near.

SILENCE IS GOLDEN

When was the last time you were silent before God? When was the last time, instead of talking to Him, you just listened to Him? This doesn't mean sitting down for five minutes without your phone. I'm talking about going into a room, shutting the door, and purposefully removing every distraction to just be still for several moments.

Scripture says, "Be still and know that I am God" (Ps. 46:10, NLT). The NASB translation reads like this: "Cease striving and know that I am God." Another alternate reading for the word *striving* can be translated: "Let go, relax."[1]

There are circumstances allowed into our lives that will bring tension and cause uncomfortable stress. In order to try to avoid the struggle, we start to sprint up a mountain, trying to clear hurdles along the way, just so we can get to the top. In our fatigued state, when our lungs won't take any more, we become depleted of all nourishment. The hurdles we're hoping to clear begin to become larger than the mountain we're trying to run and we start to make wrong decisions based on reaction instead of response.

God created rest for a purpose. He created stillness for a reason. When we learn to be intentionally silent and take the break we so desperately need, wonderful things can happen in our relationship with the One who loves us the most. When we're silent, we get the privilege of clearly hearing our Creator guide us through the rough and perilous water ahead. We then are able to build a response to His guidance rather than a reaction brought about by our fearful view that's limited because of our fallen and sinful nature. Silence truly is golden.

When we reach our breaking point and the boulders seem too great to handle, we need to draw close to the source of our strength by being quiet and still. When our problems seem insurmountable, we must stop, pull our paddles in, and let go of the controls. Christ has every capability to get us through, but we have to relax, stop screaming, stop pushing, and stop clutching to survive and simply trust. This is a discipline built by silence. This is surrender.

Jesus instructs us that in order to follow Him, we must deny ourselves. Luke 9:23 notes, "And He was saying to them all, 'If anyone wishes to come after Me, he must deny himself, and take up his cross daily and follow Me.'"

This isn't just a practice when things are out of control and we feel we've been severely misplaced. As Christ commands, it's a daily discipline. We won't gain anything by desperate commotion engaged by fear, doubt, and control. Instead, we're to deny our sinful nature so we may cling to His perfect nature.

Be encouraged. Don't allow the breaking points to split your life in two and cause you to drown in the raging waters.

Instead, quiet your mind and your soul. Then listen to Jesus, your Guide. He is going to lead you past the boulders and keep you safe so you don't drown when problems arise. As the old hymn boldly declares:

"On Christ, the solid Rock, I stand;
All other ground is sinking sand,
All other ground is sinking sand."[2]

SIX

SURRENDERED:
PRAYING WITH TRUST AND EXPECTANCY

*We tend to use prayer as a last resort, but God wants it to be our
first line of defense. We pray when there's nothing else we can do,
but God wants us to pray before we do anything at all.*
—Oswald Chambers

As we continued down course on our white-water rapids trip, a thought occurred to me: Everyone on the raft
seemed so confident and fearless. They were so anchored,
but I was oblivious. Yet again, I was the odd one out. I wanted to
be at the end of this crazy ride and was hoping we'd just magically
finish. So I continued to be in a constant state of desperation. My
screaming tirades were becoming something of the norm.

I mean, how could everyone else be so calm? Our lives were
hanging in the balance and just a second earlier, I had almost
met an untimely demise by being flung into a rock. Good
grief, people. *Stop smiling!* I thought. *This is terrible!*

Then I felt a large hand on my shoulder and, of course, I froze. This time, our guide didn't speak in the intimidating voice he previously used. Authoritative yes, but it had a peaceful tone. It was calming. "You've got to trust me," he said. "We've still got a ways to go."

My aha moment was about to arrive. I'd allowed myself to be surrounded by misguided fear and distrust. I'd solely fixed my eyes on what I could see. I honestly didn't believe our guide would be able to keep us afloat, so I had an expectation of failure. My own pride was driven by self-preservation and caused great separation, confusion, and downright terror.

Flip that to a spiritual lens. Trusting in God, His word, and unfailing promises is the first step to surrender and the foundational building block to being surrendered in prayer. Those who were on the raft with me believed in our guide and his navigation to get us down the river, no matter what we came up against. He'd done it so many times and had experienced the course in a multitude of environments, so those onboard were confident in his abilities to lead and keep us safe in the process.

When we come into the saving grace of Christ Jesus and place our trust in Him as our Lord and Savior, we're placing our trust in the Creator of the universe, the One who put the earth in orbit, perfectly set the sun and moon, and creatively spread the stars in the sky.

> In the beginning the Word already existed.
> The Word was with God,
> and the Word was God.
> He existed in the beginning with God.
> God created everything through him,

and nothing was created except through him.
The Word gave life to everything that was created,
    and his life brought light to everyone.
The light shines in the darkness,
    and the darkness can never extinguish it. . . .
He came into the very world he created, but the
world didn't recognize him.

(John 1:1–5, 10, NLT)

He knit us together in our mother's womb and has set our exact number of days on the earth (see Ps. 139:13, 16). His provisions are unmatched and His knowledge is far greater than any understanding a human could develop. We'll never be able to fathom God's process of thought and degree of comprehension. Isaiah 55:8 says, "'My thoughts are nothing like your thoughts,' says the LORD. / 'And my ways are far beyond anything you could imagine'" (NLT).

Placing our full trust in God through prayer is vital. It nurtures the incomprehensible connection we have with our Creator. This is where we learn that we can fully rely on Him and be authentic in our requests, concerns, gratitude, fears, and worries. As this foundational work builds, expectation grows because we see God navigate us through waters that with a masterful hand. Expectant prayer removes us from the realm of human limitation and takes us into the realm where the work of the supernatural is unleashed, unbound by the confines that surround us.

Expectation is intimately linked with trust. David, a man after God's own heart, said, "In the morning I will order my prayer to You and eagerly watch" (Ps. 5:3). This is the lifeline in the relationship between us and our Guide and it finely tunes our ear to His lead and His purpose. It then opens the door to His unfathomable provisions and strength.

HOW DO YOU VIEW PRAYER?

It takes a pretty serious inward look to understand what we think about prayer. Some questions to consider:

- Do you have full confidence in the God who sovereignly holds your life and your circumstances?

- Who do you believe in more? Yourself or Him?

- Who do you believe knows the exact outcome of what's ahead?

- When you pray, to what depths are you seeking out God's will versus your own?

- Do you take the time to ask and then listen to what He has to say about what you're requesting and asking?

- As a matter of even closer examination, have you asked the Lord what He would like you to request and made the time to actually hear the answer?

Take a break and answer the questions above. Be honest. Consider this profound quote from Andrew Murray: "Prayer is not monologue, but dialogue; God's voice . . . is its most essential part."[1] What does your prayer life look like? Notice

I didn't ask what your *prayers* look like but what your prayer *life* resembles.

LEARNING TO BE EXPECTANT IN PRAYER

Many of us take the access of prayer for granted. We pray before a meal, sporting event, or before we go to sleep at night. Many of us pray in a moment of crisis or when in dire need. But when it comes to the daily discipline of prayer we can't find the downtime. We're surrendered to the tasks that make up our lifestyle: our job, our fitness and health, our entertainment and hobbies, taking care of the kids and their schedules . . . the list could go on and on.

A PERSONAL STORY

My wife and I married on October 14, 2006. Being newly married, we had wonderful hopes for our future, as many couples do. We obviously wanted a full family, but weren't in any hurry. We believed it was important to build the foundation of who we were before bringing children into the mix. Taking two and melding as one takes time.

The first few years were very memorable. I learned a lot about my new bride and she learned a lot about me. As our fourth year of marriage came around, we felt God was leading us to start our family and we felt we were ready to take the next step. We didn't know what would lie ahead, but we knew we might face certain challenges in having children. Due to some intense medical complications my wife experienced in high school, there were already some underlying uncertainties (more on her story in Chapter 9), but we knew God was calling us to step forward in faith.

Many, many months went by without a positive result for pregnancy. Highly discouraged, we went through some rounds of testing to see if there might be a problem. The results came in—we weren't going to get pregnant by natural means and would need to seek out other options. This wasn't an easy addition to an already tough journey, but we believed God would provide.

I'm not consistent in journaling, but I'll write things down from time to time. As I look back on our journey and read through certain entries, I found some writings that are quite interesting and don't believe them to be coincidence. As a matter of fact, they're directly linked and intimately connected to surrender. God used my circumstances and the pleadings of my heart to shape expectant prayer and surrender in my life and my wife's as well.

Thursday, February 17
7:27 a.m.

Today I prayed that God would teach me surrender. I asked that He would be gentle in His instruction.

Be careful what you pray for! I wasn't aware of it at the time I prayed that prayer, but the journey of "becoming pregnant" was the start of the lesson I'd requested. A trust was being developed for the waters that lie ahead, but I wasn't fond of that particular brand of guiding. I remember as the months passed with no good news, I'd plead with God to do something that would encourage us. I began to wonder if the prayers were being heard at all and I went through my share of concern and worry that my requests were ceiling prayers, just floating up into the drywall, especially when there was silence for months.

However, I knew God had placed a passionate burden within our hearts. Therefore, He was calling us to trust Him, even though we couldn't physically or spiritually see evidence of the way in which He was handling the situation. This was an answer to my prayer, but not in the way I had hoped. That was hard to understand. As the husband and spiritual leader, I strived to be an example to my wife of someone who was trusting in God and His lead, even though inwardly I was struggling. We went through many months of waiting and it was only getting harder to deal with, especially as my bride struggled through deep, impacting emotions of being "incomplete."

Monday, May 9
6:31 a.m.

I have been in a lull spiritually. It's been tough to spend time with my heavenly Father. It's a unique separation. I know He is close, but I do not sense it. It's interesting.

I believe God is teaching me about "true expectation" in Him. I have prayed for a renewed freshness and vigor of great expectations in my spiritual outlook of all that God is doing.

Waiting on God can be tough. But the beautiful outcome removes us from the ownership we feel we have over what's coming to pass. Waiting also gives us strength for the stretch. God was working and was teaching me an invaluable lesson.

Thursday, June 16
6:37 a.m.

I have begun to pray the prayer that I believe God has provisioned for my wife and me in regards to children. . . . I wait with great anticipation and expectation.

But more months would follow and we'd find ourselves discouraged. The emotional and spiritual roller coaster was exhausting. There were days when all I could say to God was: "Just meet me where I am right now, 'cause that's all I got." Little did we know our hope was being grounded in the unseen.

After meeting with our doctor, she felt it was time to start a round of tests. We then received the message of finality that confirmed what we had wondered: It's not going to happen. The most interesting thing took place in the moment we received the results. We felt peace. At that point, because of the journey and lead of our true Guide, a trust had been cultivated allowing us to come to the full realization that God was in complete control and obviously knew what He was doing. We had surrendered.

We were advised to meet with our doctor and see what other options we could pursue, so we set an appointment. But God had other plans.

Wednesday, October 5
7:10 a.m.

I feel a sense of release from the prayer that God has provisioned for us about children. Not sure why. Maybe Sarah is pregnant.

Thursday, October 13
6:50 a.m.

Sarah took a pregnancy test and it has revealed that she is pregnant!

After a few weeks passed and the answer was resoundingly clear, we canceled the doctor appointment we'd set to find out about other options. It was now time to enter into the new phase of life as parents.

As we made our way down our specific river path, God taught us the unparalleled truth that expectation and trust are linked together in a profound way that moves individual and personal mountains. By His guidance and navigation, we literally watched human life come from nothing. As we expectantly called on Him, intentionally listened to Him, and continued down the course He placed before us, He changed what seemed like an impossibility.

A DAILY CONNECTION

When we live a life without the daily connection of prayer, we walk in broken fellowship with our Guide and our trust in Him will never fully develop. Philippians 4:6 gives us this instruction: "Do not be anxious about anything, but in *every situation, by prayer and petition*, with thanksgiving, *present your requests to God*" (NIV). Ephesians 6:18 also tells us to "pray in the Spirit *on all occasions* with all kinds of prayers and requests" (NIV).

Seems to be a pretty consistent theme. Do these verses give you the impression that God wants us to throw up a quick request as an afterthought? We've all done that, right? *Oh yeah, God. Sorry, forgot You were there. Umm . . . okay—help us to win this game and keep me from getting hurt. Thanks. Oh, sorry . . . amen.*

There's nothing wrong with a quick request, but when that's all we're about, our prayer life will never see the full depth of strength of what prayer can really do. Expectation cannot grow without trust, and trust can only mature by building a relationship that's watered and fertilized by consistent and intentional communication. This daily pursuit is a necessity in order to victoriously trek the river wild.

Author and minister George MacDonald wrote, "In whatever man does without God, he must fail miserably, or succeed more miserably."[2] Expectant prayer is a strength to our witness because it also conveys humility and allows God to do work through us that can take observers by surprise. When we are weak, He is strong (see 2 Cor. 12:10). We're admitting we need help and are incapable of fully carrying out what we've been charged to do. God does not despise a humble heart and with His help, our impossibilities become realities. Scripture is quite clear about this:

> Though the LORD is great, He cares for the humble,
> but He keeps His distance from the proud.
> (Ps. 138:6, NLT)

> The humble will see their God at work and be glad.
> Let all who seek God's help be encouraged.
> (69:32, NLT)

I've personally witnessed God go to work and break through what I believed to be insurmountable obstacles. This followed the times when I persistently and fervently called to Him, trusting with an expectation that He would do the impossible. In a few of those situations, not only did God do the impossible, He took the requests laid before Him and answered in a way far beyond what I could have dreamed.

OUR DEPENDENCE

We can easily take the gracious access to our Creator and Lord for granted. Learning to live in expectant prayer is essential in every believer's life. It's at this point we exchange human dependency for God dependency. Christ followers need to surrender to this kind of disciplined prayer life. Our spiritual vitality is weakened when we're in broken fellowship with our Guide. Expectant prayer keeps us securely in place.

In a world that creates delusions of peace about the capabilities of me, myself, and I, we must reverse our mind-set and completely trust in God, the Creator of every kingdom. The purpose of this sanctifying work of Christ in our lives isn't solely for our own goodness and blessing. It's for the light to shine through the utter darkness of our natural world so the supernatural can be made known to men. This is part of the saving work of Christ that by His grace, His sheep will come home. The quote from our friend Oswald Chambers is worth repeating: "We tend to use prayer as a last resort, but God wants it to be our first line of defense. We pray when there's nothing else we can do, but God wants us to pray before we do anything at all."[3] Expectant prayer keeps us in the mind-set of surrender.

SEVEN

SURRENDERED: CRAFTED PRAYER

When we finally passed through the "Can Opener"—you remember, the rapid that could have split our raft in two and hurled me straight toward the rocks of doom—we pulled over to the bank of the river. There we emptied our raft of all the water we had collected from the previous white waters we'd gone through. I was hoping to get some encouragement but instead, I got an earful from my brother. I had it coming, I suppose.

> "John! You're NOT LISTENING! Stop screaming your head off and do what the guide is telling you to do! As we battle through this, some of us can hardly hear anything 'cause you can't calm down! Man! You've almost died like twenty times!"

I have to admit it: Actually listening to our guide did cross my mind, but the thought was clearly not being put into practice. Being accused of almost dying "twenty times" is a bit of an exaggeration, but it's not too far off the mark. He was right. I needed to listen. I really, really needed to listen. My lack of practice in that matter was a tremendous hindrance and caused a lack of understanding and clarity.

We can often find ourselves treating our prayer lives the exact same way. How often do we take time to listen to what the Lord wants to say to us about what we're praying? It's easy to just throw out requests, say thanks, amen, and then move along. However, being surrendered in prayer requires us to take a break from our "wish list" and beckons an acknowledgment of what God is trying to communicate to us so that we may pray in complete alignment with Him.

This action takes time and practice, but it keeps us grounded in the continual pursuit of His word and linked intimately and relationally with Him. It unifies us with His intentions and removes our feelings of entitlement. As we seek out His righteousness, God's plan takes course and clarifies the path ahead as we learn to deny ourselves.

LISTENING

You might be wondering how exactly we can "hear" from God. For some, this might prove to be a step outside the norm and can seem difficult at first. It's easy to believe that when God has something to say, He's going to make sure it's heard by shouting it from the heavens, but Scripture gives us a different view.

In First Kings 19, Elijah is running from the wicked—and I mean wicked—Jezebel. Elijah was discouraged and quite fearful, so God decided to give him a little encouragement and told him to stand on a mountain as the Lord Himself would pass by. Elijah obeyed. I believe he was probably a little dumbfounded by the whole experience.

> Then a great and powerful wind tore the mountains apart and shattered the rocks before the LORD, but the LORD was not in the wind. After the wind there was an earthquake, but the LORD was not in the earthquake. After the earthquake came a fire, but the LORD was not in the fire. And after the fire came a gentle whisper. (1 Kings 19:11–12, NIV)

I feel like this would have been a weatherman's worst nightmare. Can you hear the personal weathercast for Elijah?

> *Greetings E! Glad you tuned in today for your personal weather watch because this is going to be like nothing you've ever seen—and, for that matter, like nothing I've ever seen either! Here's what you can expect for today: From out of nowhere, a forceful wind is going to blast right through these mountains and literally start tearing them apart. That's just phase one. Then, without any perceivable break, you're going to experience a massive earthquake. As a cave dweller, I'd recommend trying to get away from any loose rocks, but I think that's going to be impossible because you'll probably be trapped from the massive blowout you just experienced from all that wind. Then, just for you, following that earthquake, a blazing inferno is going to heat things up real nice. Watch those eyebrows! Thanks for tuning in and hey—don't get caught out in the open!*

Thinking about this makes me laugh. I can only imagine the facial expressions Elijah was making as all of this was going on. There's Elijah, so wrapped in fear that he's hiding out in a cave from a human, mere clay and bones. Then God showed up with some needed correction and illuminated His awesome power, reminding Elijah who he should really fear—the One who not only created that clay and bones, but could destroy both the body and spirit (see Matt. 10:28). It's there, in the calm, God whispered to Elijah and unfolded His plans for his continued journey.

Like Elijah, it's easy to become distracted by all the happenings around us that can catch us off guard. In my own life, I've noticed how quickly I can forget that God is sovereign, in complete control, and has no problem handling what's before me. I sometimes get frustrated when my fear returns and I want to hide. I again rely on self-dependence, even after I've watched God do the impossible and take care of a matter that, on my own, I could have never, ever handled.

The Lord's patience is astounding because more often than not, I return back to that place and find a cave to keep me safe instead of the fierce arms of my loving, protective, and caring Creator. Then God calls me out from the darkness and begins to speak softly. Crafted prayer is about tuning into His glorious and gentle whisper.

CRAFTED PRAYER

Most understand the act of what I call "spontaneous prayer." This comes quite naturally. We come before the Lord with requests because of a burden He has placed on our hearts or some deep emotion we feel or simply to bless the food that's in front of us. Spontaneous prayer is a wonderful gift, but the drive for what we're praying for can quickly fade and can lack persistence. Often in spontaneous prayer, if we're unable to see the answers we're hoping for, we move on because we become disheartened or believe "this must not be God's will."

Crafted prayer takes us beyond spontaneity. It is a prayer life based on the timeless principle of listening before you speak—listening to what the Lord has to say in light of your specific situation and praying prayers of His promise guided by His word. Through this discipline, we begin to form our prayers not as a fleeting, spontaneous hope but as persistent, passionate outpourings that consciously communicate God's will over our own.

This kind of prayer is especially helpful when we have no idea what to say. Scripture gives assurance of the promise that in these times, the Holy Spirit is interceding for us in groans that words cannot express, especially when we're unable to effectively communicate the burden on our heart. Romans 8:26 says, "In the same way the Spirit also helps our weakness; for we do not know how to pray as we should, but the Spirit Himself intercedes for us with groanings too deep for words." The Lord, through His Spirit, has given us a truly remarkable provision for when we feel we've come to a dead end. He does not abandon us when we've got nothing to offer.

Truth be told, it can be tough to stay the course in times of disillusionment, distress, worry, fear, and anxiety. And when we get discouraged, it can become easy to just stop praying and stop seeking. These emotions can be crippling and are useful to the Enemy. They can be used to drive us away from the resting place of God and into frantic commotion, which can cause the fires of faith to become simmering coals rather than a blazing furnace.

However, before we begin walking through the steps of cultivating this act of prayer, it's important to make note of some facts. This is not a "name it and claim it" approach to your prayer life, as some may teach about prayer regarding God's promises in Scripture. We're encouraged to test everything man teaches by using the Bible and seeking to understand the context of what's being taught. It's unwise to just believe everything you hear and follow it blindly. Always see if it lines up directly with God's truth, not some twisted ideal based on man's worldly desire. This is what Paul is referring to in Ephesians 4: "We are no longer to be children, tossed here and there by waves and carried about by every wind of doctrine, by the trickery of men, by craftiness in deceitful scheming" (4:14).

We are not to be tossed by every wave of doctrine. We are to act as the Bereans: "Now the Berean Jews were of more noble character than those in Thessalonica, for they received the message with great eagerness and examined the Scriptures every day to see if what Paul said was true" (Acts 17:11, NIV).

Crafted prayer is not about selfish pursuits. Prayer is not a magical cascade of words to use so that we can attain whatever we want. That's not the purpose of prayer and it's not the purpose of God's Word. We must not misconstrue it for what it is not. Second Timothy 3:16 says, "All Scripture is inspired by God and profitable for teaching, for reproof, for correction, for training in righteousness." The Bible equips us and trains us for the good work we're to carry out. It breathes life into our souls, feeds our spiritual appetites, and guides us in our prayers. When we approach the promises of God properly with sound doctrine, the miraculous can unfold and overwhelm us in the Lord's goodness and faithfulness.

It's important to have sound biblical doctrine before we start "claiming" promises we believe are from God for our lives and others. First Timothy 4:16 instructs us in this as it says, "Watch your life and doctrine closely. Persevere in them" (NIV). Seek to have the proper knowledge of what you are claiming through prayer before you start saying, "This is for me." Not every promise stated in the Bible is for every believer. For example, in Joshua 1:3, God tells Joshua, "I promise you what I promised Moses: 'Wherever you set foot, you will be on land I have given you'" (NLT). That was a specific promise given to Joshua and the Israelites for that moment in time.

It is also important to understand that crafted prayer is not about giving us freedom from our circumstance immediately. Whatever condition is before us, God is using it to shape and mold us. In some situations, that means we have to persevere in order to move forward with the destiny He has in store. We're reminded in Hebrews 12:1: "And let us run with perseverance the race marked out for us" (NIV).

Your race is your circumstance, though it may vary in different stages of life. To run it well, you need to seek after God's pursuits in action and not your own. It helps to understand that God does indeed care about our circumstance, but He cares much more about our character. This must be understood before crafted prayer becomes effective.

When the Lord provisioned the prayer of promise for me, my wife, and our firstborn, His providence was not immediate. It took time. Our trust in Him needed to go deeper and we needed to become fully aware of God's complete sovereignty and ability to work a miracle. God's pursuits revealed a deeper level of knowledge and intimacy in who He is and He wanted to communicate that to us through our experience. My way was to see it unfold quickly, without any struggle. But God wanted to go further and He wanted to refine us. I'm so glad He did because our prayer life hasn't been the same since. We expectantly cling to His promises and come to Him in greater confidence than we did before. Crafted prayer has become a valuable treasure.

REPENTANCE

So I strive always to keep my conscience clear before God and man.

Acts 24:16, NIV

Repentance is another key factor in being able to listen clearly. Daily repentance maintains a clear conscience and keeps us directly in line with our Guide. Sin makes things messy. It fogs the brain, clouds our decisions, and when left unchecked, creates a rift. God doesn't initiate the separation. As we see in the story of Adam and Eve long ago, man creates that division and our vibrant fellowship with God is broken. Remember, Adam and Eve tried to hide from God; the pure fellowship they enjoyed broke when sin became an object of affection.

Sin equals brokenness. As believers, we're not free from committing sin. We're forgiven, but we still make mistakes and are unable to see clearly. In many cases, we allow ourselves to get used to our sin even though we know it's not right.

When we pulled over to the riverbank to empty our rafts, we were clearing out anything we'd collected on the ride that was weighing us down. We had to keep our raft free from the unnecessary burden of accumulated water, twigs, and leaves. Repenting of our sin is a similar act. Sin is such a hindrance and burden that it weighs us down and weakens our ability to hear God's voice clearly and stay single-focused.

If unsure about sin in your life, follow the example of David. He said, "Search me, God, and know my heart; / test me and know my anxious thoughts. / See if there is any offensive way in me, / and lead me in the way everlasting" (Ps. 139:23–24, NIV). It's not fun admitting where we've messed up, but what I love about David's prayer is the fact that he really wanted to know. He sought out where his faults could bring him to ruin. Satan and his army tend to find our greatest weakness and work to bring us down by attacking that flaw. Asking God to reveal those areas to you only makes you stronger in the battle that rages on in the spiritual war we are involved in.

When we do fall, because of Jesus we can repent, turn away, and be strengthened again. After his sin with Bathsheba, David prayed, "Create in me a pure heart, O God, / and renew a steadfast spirit within me. . . . / Restore to me the joy of your salvation / and grant me a willing spirit, to sustain me" (51:10, 12, NIV). Known as a "man after God's own heart," David understood that the Lord could replenish and restore what had been lost through his failings. Like David, it's wise to ask our Creator where we will easily be tempted and, when we mess up, to recognize what we've done so we and those around us who have been affected can be restored.

Being specific about our sins is also important. God knows exactly what we've done, but it's essential for us to see what He sees. It's easy to blanket forgiveness and move on, but as certain sins are revealed, we need to recognize the aspects of the wrong so that we may be effective in turning from it. As a follower of Christ, you're forgiven—that debt's been paid. You're renewed daily by His blood because God's compassions are new every morning (see Lam. 3:22–23). He's faithful to forgive. John gives us this encouraging insight: "If we confess our sins, He is faithful and just and will forgive us our sins and purify us from all unrighteousness" (1 John 1:9, NIV).

However, it's a pretty strong guarantee that at some point in our waking moments, we're going to fall short. No one's beyond sin. We all make mistakes. We all have wrong motives at times. We all take wrong actions. We may think our choices aren't hurting anyone, that they only impact us, but that's simply not the truth. We struggle against selfishness every single day, which reflects itself in our relationships and brings division in our spiritual lives, which then affects our emotional, mental, and physical well-being. So we must confess our sin to bring about the rightful unity we desperately need with our heavenly Father. We all sin, as Romans 3:23 tells us, "For all have sinned and fall short of the glory of God" (NIV) and First John 1:8 says, "If we say that we have no sin, we are deceiving ourselves and the truth is not in us." Sin darkens our spiritual lens and eyesight.

Before music entered my life, I played soccer. It was a big, big part of my childhood all the way to my upper school years. I played in a very competitive league once as a teenager and I also played for my high school team. One night during a game, I was running toward a player who was dribbling the ball down the field. I thought he was going to either try to get around me or pass it off. Little did I know he was going to aim for my head and drill the ball at my face. I wasn't prepared for what happened next.

SLAM! I got pelted in the eye. My reflexes were not nearly fast enough to dodge the oncoming ball.

Now for some reason, this hit to the eye messed up my senses pretty bad. I felt like my nose had broken, everything became muffled in my ears, and, though the ball hit one eye, I went blind in both. I was known among my coaches for having a high pain tolerance and I didn't want to give away the fact that I was most definitely injured, so I kept trying to play despite the fact that I could no longer see, smell, or hear. That wasn't smart.

Next thing I knew, I was veering off the field onto the adjacent running track, calling for the ball. I was screaming, "Hey, I'm open! I'm open!" and I was confused why I was not getting a pass. Then, though quite muffled, I started to make out the sound of my coach screaming, "STANLEY! STANLEY! What are you doing?! Get back on the field!" I just stopped and stood there because I had no clue where I was and how to get back on the field, much less how to make it over to the sidelines. My vision had been completely compromised.

Sin does the same thing. It compromises our clarity and the purity of our vision and pursuits with God. Daily repentance keeps us on the right track and purges our conscience so we can make out what's good, acceptable, and perfect. It clears the way for the sensitive communion we so desperately need to live a vibrant, obedient life in full surrender. When living this way, we stay sensitive to the voice of the Holy Spirit and we're able to listen and hear Him clearly.

TAKING THE STEPS TOWARD CRAFTED PRAYER

Here's how to begin.

1. First, find a quiet place without distractions. Pray and ask the Lord to guide you through these steps. Ask Him to speak to you and pray that He transforms your mind to see any circumstance as He does.

   Take some time to think about the situations in your life that have control over you. What seems to be dominating your life or even part of your life? Where do you feel defeated and hopeless? Are there issues causing anxiety, worry, and fear? Is there something that stirs lust within your heart that you're unable to break free from? No matter what it might be, seek it out. Even small things can count big.

2. Write down how you feel about those circumstances as if you were having a conversation with the Lord. If there's not a glaring issue at hand, this might take some time, so be patient. Ask the Lord what He sees, and listen. As certain matters are brought to mind, write them down conversationally as requests to God in how you feel about each of these issues.

   • Are you angry? Are you angry with *Him*?

   • Do these circumstances stir up emotions? Which ones?

   • Are you hurt?

It's critical to understand as believers that honesty with God is important. He already knows your thoughts before a word is on your tongue, so be real with Him (see Ps.139:4). In this practice of honesty, it's important to point out the difference between stating your emotions versus keeping a forward focus on your emotions. Avoid allowing your feelings to surround your prayers. When we concentrate on our feelings—especially depression, hate, unforgiveness, and anger—we can easily lose heart all over again. State how you feel and then move on. Don't linger in self-pity.

3. After you lay yourself bare before God, ask Him to show you promises in His word that deal with your specific situation. He can use whatever He wants to get these promises through to you. He'll certainly use Scripture, but He can also use people who speak His wisdom into your life, or a program, a sermon, a word on television or the radio. As we've discussed, don't just recklessly believe whatever comes your way. Test the word brought into your life. Take it back to Him and ask for complete confirmation. In this interval, learn to give thanks to God for His sovereignty in your life and let that thankfulness resonate in your spirit. He's in control of it all.

4. When the Lord begins to reveal His promises to you, write them down. Then begin to formulate your prayers around His promises. Repent of any sin that's been keeping you locked up: unnecessary worry, fear, fretting, withholding forgiveness, bitterness, rage, anger, hate, lust, or anything else that's been a hindrance in your walk with the Lord and in your prayer life.

5. Write down your simple prayer of thanksgiving, something that truly resonates deep within your spirit. It doesn't have to be long. God loves a thankful heart and when we operate in a grateful mind-set, we're redirected and set on the right path, guided by His supernatural wisdom.

6. Then take the promises and scriptural wisdom He has placed in front of you and articulate them in a prayer you can lay before the Lord on a regular basis. Express yourself naturally, as you would to a family member or friend. God doesn't care how grammatically correct our prayers are. He cares about the deep communication of the hungering heart. Whatever conveys the deepest longing within you is the best approach. God loves the passionate prayers of His saints as James tells us, "The earnest prayer of a righteous person has great power and produces wonderful results" (James 5:16, NLT).

7. As this prayer takes shape, the final step is persistence. Lay it before the Lord daily. Pray until you see results. The answer may not come the way you feel it should or exactly how you want, but rest assured it will come.

This entire process takes time, but that's okay. Remember, you're learning a new skill on this adventurous river ride called life and foundational development is key. You're building the discipline of listening and, just like any learned skill, growth is not immediate. The practice has to be daily. As you rely on God's truth, you'll come to understand His leading in a way you've never known before. Your mind will be transformed by

His word, His promises, and His direction. You'll begin to value your circumstance, identifying the growth that's occurring through patience.

Crafted prayer brings peace and strength in the resting place of God. His armor will cover you and His comfort and hope with strengthen you. Ephesians 6:13–18 says:

> Therefore, take up the full armor of God, so that you will be able to resist in the evil day, and having done everything, to stand firm. Stand firm therefore, HAVING GIRDED YOUR LOINS WITH TRUTH, and HAVING PUT ON THE BREASTPLATE OF RIGHTEOUSNESS, and having shod YOUR FEET WITH THE PREPARATION OF THE GOSPEL OF PEACE; in addition to all, taking up the shield of faith with which you will be able to extinguish all the flaming arrows of the evil one. And take THE HELMET OF SALVATION, and the sword of the Spirit, which is the word of God. With all prayer and petition pray at all times in the Spirit.

Crafted prayer isn't always necessary. However, it's a wonderful discipline to enact when you've hit a wall of despair and hopelessness and you don't know what or how to pray. God gives us His promises to strengthen our hope and connection with Him. His Word is our very foundation as Christ followers and He doesn't lie (see Num. 23:19; Heb. 6:18). Crafted prayer links us to his unfailing Word and His will.

DENY WHAT EASILY HINDERS

He must set his heart to conquer by prayer, and that will mean
that he must first conquer his own flesh, for it is the flesh that
hinders prayer always.

—A.W. Tozer

Being surrendered in prayer won't always be an easy discipline but it's well worth the time and sacrifice. It lays a foundation for an eternal treasure that far outweighs any personal gain you'll experience on this earth. Yes, you'll see great benefits in the here and now, but it doesn't end on this ground. Don't let your flesh hinder your prayer life.

Christ has made a way for us to have a wonderfully intimate relationship with our heavenly Father and prayer nurtures this amazing communion. I urge you to take the time to make this a priority. Intentionally pursue this connection with Him who is able to do immeasurably more than you or I can think or even imagine. Build upon it as any solid relationship is built: by listening before speaking.

EIGHT

WHAT DO YOU COUNT AS REAL SUCCESS?

Initially, when our bus pulled up to the river and we started to exit, one thought continually pressed into my mind: I literally have no idea what I'm doing. I'd not gone to school to learn how to successfully raft down death-defying white water. My hobbies didn't circulate around the interest either. This was the first of its kind for me.

The truth is, it was the first white-water rafting trip for the majority of people there. The guides were really the only ones who knew what to do and had enough experience and knowledge to train us on the fly. Interesting to note, not one single person turned back, however. No one reboarded the bus because they felt unqualified and didn't know what they were doing. They were willing and ready, come what may. The calling of God can be very similar.

A WORD TO PARENTS, GRANDPARENTS, AND GUARDIANS

It's natural to want the best for our children, but there are some principal truths you need to remember. Your children or other individuals under your influence are not you. They weren't created to fulfill a dream you might have missed out on. They weren't created to assure you have a promised retirement or to take care of matters you think are essential for your fulfillment.

What is imperative is that they follow God's directive for their lives, not man's. You need to make sure, as a spiritual leader and principal influence, that you guide them to their calling and purpose, even if that means you meet certain criticisms or become unpopular in your community, even in your church family. God's call and direction for them is important and too much is at stake for them to be guided elsewhere.

Fathers, there's within us a tendency to project our dreams and visions for our lives onto our kids. God's design for you is usually not His design for your child. It may not be God's plan for your son or daughter to be the best at a sport, have a law degree from Harvard, or even finish college. That may frustrate you or possibly scare you.

Particularly in the field of music, I've been surprised at how many leaders either went to college for only a year or two or never went at all. Some of them have gone on to win Academy Awards and Grammys. Some have made groundbreaking contributions and are hailed as musical geniuses.

My decision to leave college did not come easy and it was not a celebrated thought for my parents either at first. My father had been through years of school and worked hard to earn two master's degrees. My mother graduated from college and was a teacher at the time. My brother, cousins, aunts, uncles, and friends were all either college graduates or heading in that direction. For them, that's the path that was best, but God had something different in mind for me.

Every single created individual has an identifiable purpose. God doesn't do "cookie-cutter." His choices and course for your child may not be the path you or your friends and family were guided through. Don't measure your child's success by comparison. This is an important principle to remember. As the spiritual leader in your home, it's essential to be watchful and prayerful about how you direct your children because your guidance is critical. Encouraging them to follow God's instruction to fulfill the purpose they were created for is your utmost priority. Please remember this one thing, if nothing else from this book: **How your children view you is how they will ultimately view their heavenly Father.** Maintain focus on what's vital for their lives, not just what's important to you.

It's a tragedy to think of those who've missed a great calling because they've been shamed, grieved with guilt, and pressed into something they weren't meant to be. What's at stake is the kingdom of God, not the kingdom of man.

Colossians 1:9–12 gives us a clear insight into how we can pray for our children and each other as we encourage God's ordained purpose to be fulfilled in each one of us.

> For this reason also, since the day we heard of it, we have not ceased to pray for you and to ask that you may be filled with the knowledge of His will in all spiritual wisdom and understanding, *so that you will walk in a manner worthy of the Lord, to please*

*Him in all respects, bearing fruit in every good work
and increasing in the knowledge of God;* strengthened
with all power, according to His glorious might, for
the attaining of all steadfastness and patience; joy-
ously giving thanks to the Father, who has qualified
us to share in the inheritance of the saints in Light.

Prayerfully consider how you can encourage your child or
those under your influence in their walk with the Lord. Pray
for discernment and wisdom in how to teach them to surrender to God. A consistent prayer I pray in my role as a father to
my children is, "Lord, make me successful to see in them what
you have purposed for their life. Give me wisdom and discernment to see where you have gifted them that I may help train
them in the way they should go that they may please You and
bear fruit worthy of the calling You have placed upon them."

TO ALL CHRIST-FOLLOWERS

Each of us needs to encourage one another in our practice
of faith, especially those under our influence. As a husband
or wife, encourage and pray for your spouse diligently. Inspire
your children or those in your care and pray for them consistently. As brothers and sisters in Christ, reassure one another
with a spirit of unity.

Our approach should be as follows:

Therefore if there is any encouragement in Christ,
if there is any consolation of love, if there is any fellowship of the Spirit, if any affection and compassion, make my joy complete by being of the same

mind, maintaining the same love, united in spirit, intent on one purpose. Do nothing from selfishness or empty conceit, but with humility of mind regard one another as more important than yourselves; do not merely look out for your own personal interests, but also for the interests of others. (Phil. 2:1–4)

God has trusted us to help mobilize His church, not stamp it out. This world has enough naysayers. We have enough people criticizing the church and the people of God. So with a spirit of humility, let's encourage and pray for one another as a unified body so the people of God's church can be vibrant and take ownership of who God created us to be.

USE. INFLUENCE. INSPIRE.

Every believer is equipped with spiritual and natural gifts to be used by God for God. In regard to our spiritual gifts, we're told in First Peter 4:10: "As each one has received a *special* gift, employ it in serving one another as good stewards of the manifold grace of God."

We're responsible for how we engage our gifts—spiritual and natural. We are required to use them to inspire those in our realm of influence for the kingdom of God. They were not given arbitrarily, but by divine design to fulfill a purpose.

Christ gives us a direct parable that deals with how we're to respond with the gifts and abilities He gives us. Read this modern translation of the passage commonly referred to as the parable of the talents from Matthew 25:14–29.

For it will be like a man going on a journey, who called his servants and entrusted to them his property. To one he gave five talents, to another two, to another one, to each according to his ability. Then he went away. He who had received the five talents went at once and traded with them, and he made five talents more. So also he who had the two talents made two talents more. But he who had received the one talent went and dug in the ground and hid his master's money. Now after a long time the master of those servants came and settled accounts with them. And he who had received the five talents came forward, bringing five talents more, saying, "Master, you delivered to me five talents; here, I have made five talents more." His master said to him, "Well done, good and faithful servant. You have been faithful over a little; I will set you over much. Enter into the joy of your master." And he also who had the two talents came forward, saying, "Master, you delivered to me two talents; here, I have made two talents more." His master said to him, "Well done, good and faithful servant. You have been faithful over a little; I will set you over much. Enter into the joy of your master." He also who had received the one talent came forward, saying, "Master, I knew you to be a hard man, reaping where you did not sow, and gathering where you scattered no seed, so I was afraid, and I went and hid your talent in the ground. Here, you have what is yours." But his master answered him,

"You wicked and slothful servant! You knew that I reap where I have not sown and gather where I scattered no seed? Then you ought to have invested my money with the bankers, and at my coming I should have received what was my own with interest. So take the talent from him and give it to him who has the ten talents. For to everyone who has will more be given, and he will have an abundance. But from the one who has not, even what he has will be taken away" (ESV).

There's a very specific reason why you're here. You need to find out what that is and it starts by employing what God has entrusted to you. Whatever the direction may be, it's what's right for your life, no matter what the world may say. Listen to the encouragement of godly counsel in your life, as God will use these voices to help bring clarity to the course that lies ahead.

However, be very cautious in who you trust to give you life-changing guidance. Sometimes your friends and even family may mean very well, but they can be spiritually disconnected so their discernment lacks credibility. In the overall picture, you're the one held responsible.

This takes serious consideration. We tend to overlook these factors because we're led astray by what the world says is important and we can easily miss the placement God has for us. Don't let worldly wisdom and the beliefs of the culture and society that surround you squeeze you into the wrong mold. Depend wholly on the guidance of God and you won't waste your life.

Sometimes that means boarding the raft and heading in a direction you've never been trained to handle and it seems catastrophic for your future. Along the way, you're certain to hear people tell you it's impossible. But when our eyes are opened to see the course ahead as God does, our steps of faith will guide us to a glorious treasure as we listen and obey. Proverbs 3:5 teaches us this very truth: "Trust in the LORD with all your heart / *And do not lean on your own understanding.*"

Being a success with God doesn't always involve the "typical road." What truly matters is taking the gifts He's so lavishly given, using them to bear much fruit, and entrusting Him with the details to complete the good work He's set in place. Your credentials don't qualify you for the race—God does.

Not long after Sarah and I were married, God planted a desire on my heart to write a book. I really didn't take the initial thought too seriously because, in all reality, English was one of my worst subjects in high school and college. I even had a college professor write on a literary essay of mine, "You're really not too good at this, are you?" You may frown at that, but you know what? It was true! I was a terrible writer. So when the idea first hit my mind, I really wasn't sure it was the Lord stirring that call within me. I jotted a few ideas down but did not go much further.

A few years later, I decided to do some writing on a blog. It surprised me that what I wrote started connecting with people to some degree, but that was as far as I really wanted to go with it. Literary writing just wasn't my thing.

Soon after I started the blog, I was at a family gathering for the holidays, having a discussion with my uncle. He asked me if I had ever thought about writing a book. I laughed and said it had been a thought, but I had no idea where to start or what to do. Then laughingly, I made mention of the discouraging word from my college professor.

He chuckled but quickly moved on and asked a question. "You can't answer this with 'time.' So with that in mind, what's the one thing that would prevent you from writing a book?" My answer was "I don't know how." And that's the truth. I was clueless. He encouraged me to figure it out.

Then one evening a few years ago, I was at dinner with some friends and a buddy of mine randomly made mention of a post I had recently published on the blog. He said, "Have you ever thought about writing a book?" My specific response was, "Huh?" Then I said more seriously, "Some, but nothing much past that."

Well, at that point I would have been foolish to not think that God was trying to tell me something. So I talked it over with Sarah and we began to commit it to prayer. Not long after, ideas began to surface for chapters and a theme.

Still, the thought of the task was overwhelming to say the least. I mean, writing a whole book? That's a lot of time and effort. I had a ton of questions as well. How do I format it? Do I even have enough material to make it more than two or three chapters? When am I going to have the time to even write that much? And still, the thought continued to emerge: I have no idea what I'm doing.

The more I thought about that, the more questionable it became as well. What credentials did I really have? I didn't finish college and English classes had always been a nightmare. Even more than that, as mentioned, I was told that I wasn't a good writer. I was on staff at a church, but I was not an ordained pastor, and to me, an ordained pastor seemed to be required to write a book on Christian living. The skill set that I was known for was in music, not in preaching, teaching, or any kind of literary writing except for the few who'd read the blog from time to time. I really had nothing. So as those thoughts churned, my good friend fear started to rise once again.

Once fear hit me in full effect, I stopped writing. I stopped thinking about it, despite the conviction to keep going. Then God decided to grab my attention once again. I was reading through a book by Mark Batterson called *The Circle Maker*. He was talking about God's calling and paying attention to what He purposes for your life. Then he used an example about writing a book, saying that if God has called you to write a book, then you just need to start writing.

I couldn't believe it. I laughed and said under my breath, "Okay, okay. I get it." That evening when I came home from work, I mentioned what I had read to Sarah. Then I asked if she would be willing to pray with me once again about writing a book and the possibility of having it published. Being the amazing wife she is, so patient through my back-and-forth, she agreed and began to cheer me on. We started praying about it consistently. I began to dedicate a lot of time to writing and, a year later, I had finished a very rough draft.

With no idea about what to do next, I asked that God would begin to guide the direction and details to move things forward, and He did just that. A friend and pastor on staff at Second who is quite familiar with the process began explaining to me what would need to be involved in order for publishing to take place. When the discussion was over, I walked away saying, "Well, that was a fun pipe dream, 'cause I'm pretty sure that's not gonna happen." But the Lord continued to press in.

I prayerfully began to take the next steps. Much to my surprise, a few months later, I had signed with an agent, but the process of writing had really just begun. I still had a lot to learn as well and apparently, the Lord wanted to teach me a few more life lessons that could be applied in the writing of the book before all was said and done.

The process of signing with an agent and submission to potential publishers took almost two years. A lot of life events happened during that time that hit our family hard emotionally, mentally, and spiritually. Those events taught us all the more about what surrender looks like in different seasons, whether in complete heartbreak or overwhelming joy.

Once signed with my publisher, the process of learning wasn't over. Writing a book and publishing a book are two different things, and to be completely honest, it takes some seriously hard work and thick skin. Though my knowledge of both was virtually nonexistent, God placed people in my life who taught me the how-to along the way, and He pushed me past my limitations. God was teaching me as the process evolved and qualifying the work of what He had called me into as He prepared the way.

GOD WILL QUALIFY YOU

In ancient Hebrew culture, a hierarchy divided individuals and families into different social rankings, also known as a "social class." Each class experienced different benefits and varying levels of respect. At the top of the hierarchical pyramid were men of powerful position and influence of which other social ranks came under.[1,2]

These men were kings, officials, military and civil officers, rabbis, state leaders, and heads of economically wealthy families. Special knowledge, education, and training were very important in many of these offices and those who were wealthy had their share of prominence within the hierarchy. Family history and position were important to how a person was viewed in society and had a great impact on the influence that individual would have in the social order that surrounded them.[3,4]

After the highest rank of influence came the next social class, which was the common and civilized citizens. They worked what would be considered "normal jobs" and maintained them at a proper and suitable level. Though their influence was not as powerful as those at the top of the hierarchy, they were still highly regarded and carried quite a bit of responsibility for the betterment of society.

At the bottom of the social hierarchy were the slaves. They had no responsibilities and no control over what they could do and the destiny of their lives. Most of the time, this status was inherited and individuals were born into the class, but there were instances of convicted criminals becoming slaves to serve out their punishments.[5,6]

When Christ arrived on the earth, He began to turn the tables of proper social structures and their influence on society. He did this not only through His chosen followers, but by His physical example. Jesus as God humbled Himself and became human. His earthly father was a carpenter, as was Jesus Himself. Seven of the twelve disciples were common fishermen and one was a despised tax collector. Yet those men, through the charge of their Savior, helped to change the world and had a profound impact on the society of their day and countless centuries beyond. Christ qualified them, the Holy Spirit empowered them, and the work they were called to do is still going and will continue until Jesus' return. Talk about influence! When we take a look at our society as it is today, there are some drastic differences, but much of our social hierarchy is mirrored in similar rankings. The top of our pyramid contains rulers of countries, high-ranking military officers, religious officials, men and women of higher education, and those who have a great deal of financial wealth. Then we have our middle and lower classes.

For the vast majority, our perception of the importance of these individuals is based off of what we see with our eyes. The glamour of their influence and perceived power can cause us to place a great deal of prominence on the wealth and knowledge of the world to see success only obtained through such positions and ranks. However, the eyes of our Creator see beyond what we observe. God sees society and the people that comprise it as they really are (see 1 Sam. 16:7). He sees their hearts and motives, and gives us this word of wisdom through King Solomon when looking at the reality of life among His creation: "The fastest runner doesn't always win the race, and the strongest warrior doesn't always win the battle. The wise sometimes go hungry, and the skillful are not necessarily wealthy. And those who are educated don't always lead successful lives" (Eccles. 9:11, NLT).

The Lord used Solomon to give us great insight and wisdom to reverse our mind-set. We need—and should pray for—a transformation of our minds and renewed vision. For followers of Christ, surrendering to God's lead, whatever that may be, is vital to true success, even if it's unpopular in our culture and society. We never know what God is doing with the seeds He is using us to plant. God may very well call you to go the distance and receive your doctorate. But He also may call you to drop everything, move to another country, and live in a mud-hut to use your gifts in the way He intended. The point is, your life's work and success are not dependent on the value of man's opinion and what man might consider successful. They're dependent on the value of your obedience to God's truth and conviction to what He's given you to do. It all comes back to surrender. That's true and real success.

When we move in the direction of God's call on our lives, the Lord will begin to train us and prepare us for this journey. He won't turn His back as we move toward Him. He's waiting for us to step into His influence so we can reach the potential of our purpose. God is the One who makes us suitable for the requirements ahead. After all, it's His work to be accomplished.

FARMER TURNED PROPHET

Amos is an encouraging biblical example to review when it comes to observing mere human credentials versus divine qualification. In the higher view of society, Amos wasn't much. He was a herdsman and a cultivator of sycamore trees when God called him to be a prophet. He wasn't even an official member of the Jewish religion or political institution. And yet, God used him as His very own spokesman.

When Amos began to pronounce judgment on Israel, you know there were probably quite a few people who thought he was a total fool. But God searches the earth for the hearts that are devoted to Him so He can strengthen and support them (see 2 Chron. 16:9). He'll use anyone He deems worthy because He knows what's within them. As pastor and Bible teacher Warren Wiersbe explains, "If an untrained rustic farmer is preaching God's Word, it means God has called him."[7] Amos was doing what he was created to do. Amos didn't choose this as his job—God chose it for him. Amos said, "I was neither a prophet nor the son of a prophet, but I was a shepherd, and I also took care of sycamore-fig trees. But the LORD took me from tending the flock and said to me, 'Go, prophesy to my people Israel'" (Amos 7:14–15, NIV).

Throughout history, we see God use a range of individuals to serve His church. In biblical times, He used an educated man like Moses, a shepherd like David, a warrior like Joshua, and a murderer of Christians like Saul turned Paul. When we look at church history, D.L. Moody was a shoe salesman, John Bunyan crafted pots and pans, Charles Spurgeon was too young to preach, and C.S. Lewis was a pious atheist. When the Lord captures hearts, He takes those who are surrendered to Him, equips them, and sends them out to do His great work until the return of Christ. That's powerful.

The story of Amos encourages those who feel they're not qualified to accomplish what God has placed on their hearts, despite criticism and lack of educational training or experience. As he intentionally crafted his relationship with God, Amos was given everything he needed to be successful at what God asked of him. In the midst of surrendering to God's call, Amos was also taught by God—the greatest teacher of all— and he became successful in carrying out His purpose and design.[8]

THRIVING IN GOD'S KINGDOM

Remember that this world is passing away. We don't belong here. To put our worth in a place that will soon be gone is foolish and it stirs discontentment rooted in selfishness and pride.

We can either arrogantly boast of our earthly treasure or we can let it go, humbling ourselves to serve God's greater purpose for the treasure of His kingdom. One will last, one will not. One pursuit brings contentment, the other will find us continually trying to climb a ladder of unsatisfied success. Paul says, "I have learned to be content whatever the circumstances. . . . I can do all this through him who gives me strength" (Phil. 4:11, 13, NIV).

We find lasting contentment and joy when we take our God-given talents and surrender them to Him for success that goes beyond earthly treasure and worth. When we operate in that mind-set, we learn to be satisfied in all circumstances because we're thriving in God's design for our lives. Jesus said, "Every branch in Me that does not bear fruit, He takes away; and every branch that bears fruit, He prunes it so that it may bear more fruit" (John 15:2). No matter what path is ahead of you, if God has called you into it, He will give you the instruction and training to see it through.

Don't bury your gifts and be pressed into someone you're not called to be just because that's the way everyone else does it. Allow the Lord to push you beyond your limits and be a bold follower of Christ instead of playing it safe. Our heavenly Father finds great joy in pruning our lives so we can bear much fruit. Solomon sums up our aim as children of God. When we're focused on this one thing, we'll prosper in His kingdom. This is real success: "Now all has been heard; / here is the conclusion of the matter: / Fear God and keep His commandments, / for this is the duty of all mankind" (Eccles. 12:13, NIV).

What is God calling of you? It's time to surrender.

NINE

SURRENDER IN SUFFERING

For the final time, we pulled over to the riverbank and emptied water that had collected in the raft. As we sat, taking a much-needed break, we looked ahead at the last set of white waters we would have to endure. It was by far the worst. Our guide rearranged our seating assignments, placing the adults on the outer edges and me and my brother in the middle of the raft. We were seated between our protectors because the last part of this course was deadly and we'd need every ounce of security to ensure our survival.

One by one, we watched those who went before us. When passing through the "Ocoee Gorge," the name of this specific rapid, we saw the rafts climb, then fall on the water at an almost 90-degree angle. That happened multiple times.

While we stared wide-eyed at what we were seeing, the guide informed us that if we fell out of the raft at the point of entry, we wouldn't survive. He wasn't joking. It was the first time I noticed any sort of concern in the eyes of my parents.

They didn't expect something so perilous on our family river adventure, but there we were and we had to take the plunge.

As we began to ready ourselves for the last big push, the strong words of the guide prepared us for what was coming.

> Once we hit the first peak of water, bring your paddles in. Do not place them in the water. Those on the edges, lean to the inside of the raft and sway to the direction of the water thrust. Those in the middle, don't turn to the left or to the right and keep your head straight. Secure your feet and hold on tight! Here we go.

Every emotion flooded my spirit in about ten seconds. I didn't know what to do. This seemed to be more than I could handle. But it didn't matter, because we were already moving down course. It was time for me to release any control I felt I had over what was about to occur and completely trust our guide.

In reflection, a strong parallel is present for me when I consider the times we all must endure suffering and hardships. Sometimes we can see what's ahead but in most cases, we have no idea what to expect. There's a hope we'll get through it, but we're not sure exactly how that'll happen. In times like these, God's protection abounds. We may not always be able to sense His covering but it's there, keeping us close to Him so we're not alone.

As we persevere, God surrounds us with His church to strengthen us and help keep us together when we feel we're going to fall apart. His love can be overwhelming during these periods but His love can also feel very distant. Battered and torn, we feel hope is slipping away and our tears express feelings beyond words as we cry out for rescue.

If you're going through an indescribably tough time, walking through an unparalleled struggle, or have hit a point of tragedy in your life, I am so sorry. I pray this chapter encourages you and brings a new hope that reminds you: He is faithful! Surrender in suffering is never promised to be easy, but there's a treasure of the purest kind entrusted to you. As you endure, this treasure will be revealed. Hold on and remember that God is near.

The testimonies of others help to carry us forward. When we're in a time of deep struggle, they inspire us and bring a strength provisioned by our heavenly Father. So there are two stories I'd like to share with you. They're the testimonies of two very special and strong women: my wife and my mom. In this life, they've walked through such intense trials of fire and still stand to exclaim God is faithful. He is faithful to His word, He is faithful to rescue, and He's faithful in creating hope through His overwhelming love, even amid the darkest of circumstances.

Meet Sarah and Ruby. Both have learned—and are still learning—what it means to surrender in suffering. Their stories are inspiring in more ways than one. They tell of a hope renewed every single day as they continue to deal with the circumstances that test their minds, wills, and emotions. Their lives are a reflection of the Lord's kind presence and overwhelming strength, and communicate a depth of His love that the wisdom of the world will never understand. They have a peace that wraps around them and a joy that radiates wealth that goes beyond any earthly treasure.

These two ladies "get it" and that's why I believe you'll be encouraged in reading their stories. Not only do they talk the talk, but they walk in a very close and warm relationship with their Creator and Guide, one that could not exist without the trials they've endured.

RUBY'S STORY

The love story of Douglas and Nellie Hinson is one for the silver screen. A young soldier stationed in the Panama Canal Zone at Fort Gulick during the Korean Conflict, Douglas met and fell in love with a beautiful girl from Guatemala nicknamed "Nellie" by her family and friends. After some time of passionate dating, they were married and Ruby was born shortly thereafter. After being discharged from the military, Douglas moved the new family across the border and they began living their dream on a small, quaint farm in Rusk, Texas. All was well in their world.

There was always adventure growing up in the woods of East Texas. Living on a farm, there was usually something to do. As a child, Ruby learned early how to skin a chicken, feed animals, and cook a meal for the family. With a firm, high-spirited mother and a hardworking, compassionate, loving father, the Hinson family was starting to make their way toward the American dream.

On the morning of August 17, 1963, Douglas called for Ruby to get in the car. They had to pick up Nellie from Dallas and drive her home after she and her in-laws had been visiting Douglas' brother in the VA hospital. Along with Nellie, Ruby's grandmother (her namesake) would make the trip home with the little family.

Heading back to Rusk, they began their drive down the old two-lane Highway 80 near Kaufman, Texas. Ruby was asleep in her mother's lap. A bridge overpass was up ahead and an eighteen-wheeler cattle truck was crossing. But the trucker had been drinking and, disoriented, he smashed head-on into the car carrying the Hinson family. Only Ruby survived. She was just nine years old.

Her next memory was waking up as she was being rushed through the ER and waking up again in a cold hospital room alone. In a matter of seconds, Ruby had lost everything in her world. She'd never again know the comfort of her mother's lap, the strong embrace of her father, or the loving touch of her grandmother. She was now an orphan. These dark realities would soon take their grip as she struggled to comprehend a truth no child should ever have to grasp.

One day, Ruby awoke to the sound of weeping. It was her aunt, her father's only sister, who was now Ruby's caretaker. As the day progressed, the doctors and nurses who'd been caring for her came together to tell Ruby the news of her parents' death, to which she responded, "I know."

It would seem, in a moment like this, utter darkness would surround the loneliness of the time. However, Ruby recalls sensing something a little different.

> I knew I was in someone's care. As I look back now, I know there were angels and beings that I could not see that were taking care of me. I knew the care of the heavenly Father was there. The awareness of His presence was strong, even at nine years old.

From that point on, Ruby began a journey with the glaring acknowledgment and realization that she would live this life alone. Living with an aunt and uncle who were purposefully distant, Ruby was often emotionally abused and experienced physical mistreatment at times. Even among family, she felt like an alien. As physical ties grew distant, spiritual ties with her heavenly Father became everything. Psalm 68:5 developed into an intimate reality for her: "A Father to the fatherless . . . / is God in His holy dwelling" (NIV).

> Just two months after moving in with my new family, I made a profession of faith at a James Robinson revival. He spoke of trusting the Father the way a child trusts their dad. He spoke of a child standing on a house and jumping carefree into the arms of an earthly father because of trust and how that child could trust God this same way. When the invitation came, I moved without hesitation out of the pew and down the aisle. If God was like my dad, then I knew I wanted to jump into His arms. That public profession was the confirmation of what had already been going on with my heavenly Dad and me.
>
> Through all of the emotional abuse and a couple of physical beatings, I just knew I was not alone. I clung to my heavenly Father and spent hours with friends, in Sunday school, Training Union, choir, and youth group. The teen years were tough.

Even as her faith grew, emotional chains became bondage in a spiritual and mental prison. Fear and anxiety became a new normal. Some days it would be more intense than others, bearing a weight that wasn't easy to overcome. Ruby reflects, "Fear and anxiety have been my companions for years. This has taken a toll on me. I believe God, but at times I have been overwhelmed before I trusted. God has been so patient."

As she grew older, these struggles continued to be a haunting presence. Marrying at twenty years old, those struggles remained and would reveal themselves through different circumstances, with the commitment of marriage adding complexities in sometimes unexpected ways.

Nevertheless, Ruby found great comfort in the Scriptures and still does to this day. Familiar verses guided her to the resting place of God and kept her strong in the most despairing circumstances. Not only did they give peace but God's word also protected her when the struggles seemed too great. Here are a few of her favorites:

> Be still, and know that I am God.
>
> (Ps. 46:10, NIV).

> He makes my feet like the feet of a deer;
>> He causes me to stand on the heights.
>
> (18:33, NIV)

> Because I rescued the poor who cried for help,
>> and the fatherless who had none to assist them.
>
> (Job 29:12, NIV)

As her identity in the Father grew, His strength became radiant in her weakness. A transformation began to take place and Ruby connected with the sufferings of Christ like never before.

> I knew I was His and I came to understand the meaning of "why not me?" If He [Christ] suffered as He did, then why not me? My suffering drew me close to Him because I could sense just a tiny bit of His suffering and I felt privileged to be able to communicate with Him at that level. I don't like the aloneness thread that has run throughout my life but I don't think Jesus liked it much either.

Through such an intimate connection, God has used Ruby to spread a beautiful fragrance of His hope to souls in need of encouragement and a love that goes beyond human comprehension. The Lord has richly blessed such faith. She has now been married for forty years and has two sons who cherish their mother deeply. As the younger of those two sons, I've been in awe of God's faithfulness in her life. Her walk with the Lord will be a lasting legacy carried forward into eternity through the glorious riches of Christ.

Although she hasn't had an earthly father since she was a child, the presence of her heavenly Father is genuinely valued and their relationship is one that has been deeply developed because of the loss she experienced.

> Being in the midst of mountains, hills, rivers, and streams draws me close to the Father. I love sitting, floating, hiking, and just being still with Him,

smack in the middle of His creation. It's a safe, happy place for me. He draws me to Him and I feel so joyful.

This is hope—hope in the unseen and life abundant through surrender. Ruby's treasure has been found in the One whose love is boundless and limitless beyond compare. What a mighty God we serve.

SARAH'S STORY

I remember when I first met Sarah. Her beauty blew me away. I think the first word out of my mouth when I saw her was, "Whoa." A few weeks later, I actually got the courage to ask her out on a date and now, well, the rest is history, as the phrase goes. She said "yes" to the daring question in my proposal and we've now been married for eleven years and have two wonderful children.

That doesn't seem like much out of the ordinary, nothing substantially different than your typical love story. However, there's a miracle to it. Sarah, at one point in her life, was told marriage was not an option, much less children. As a matter of fact, she was told the daily operations of life you and I take for granted every single day were not going to be the norm for her. She had a new normal and it certainly wasn't going to be easy.

It all started one afternoon during her sophomore year of high school. She woke up like every other day, got dressed, and readied herself for school, not knowing that in a few hours, her life would be drastically altered. As she was sitting in class, an intense burning sensation flared on her skin. It felt like her body was on fire from the inside.

Not able to stay at school, Sarah was picked up by her mother and taken to the doctor, only to hear, "We can't find anything wrong." It began a chain of events that would make that defeating phrase a repetitive challenge in Sarah's life. For the next year, she was poked, prodded, and studied by doctors from the nation's finest medical practices.

As the year progressed, more and more symptoms began to develop while controlled bodily functions were disabled. Sarah would drool, sweat profusely, and experience shortness of breath. Her heart rate would suddenly escalate. Fainting spells would occur, her left eye drooped, and extreme headaches increased day by day while the burning sensation remained. Doctor after doctor could not provide answers and every test came back normal.

At sixteen, living in the teenage years where appearance and perception is ostensibly everything, Sarah was forced to walk around school with IV drips while the symptoms continued to drag her down. Abandoned by once close friends who sought to manipulate peers by rumors and lies, the deception became an added emotional stress in a struggled will for survival. Everything was breaking down and hope was a distant road cut off by loneliness, rejection, depression, worry, anxiety, anger, bitterness, and a loss of any sense of normality.

Unanswered questions plagued her mind. What was all of this for? Why were there no answers? Why was there pain and hurting? What was the point of such intense suffering? If God's the great Healer, then why was He not listening and acting on the request for deliverance?

More and more the struggles of the mind, will, and emotions grew and the Enemy was preparing for a feast. Sarah would be just another notch in the belt of these wicked battles. The pictures drawn by such vile deceit became a disheartening sore in the mind's eye. Instead of seeing the truth of God's compassion and care, God was seen as the One with a magnifying glass purposely burning Sarah with each passing moment. He wasn't a loving Father but a dominating dictator whose constant answer was "no."

The hurt of such an image was more than she could take. Beating her fists on the floor, Sarah began to weep uncontrollably. This had gone far enough and she was through, but God was not. In that desperate stage, where every ounce of hope had deteriorated, Jesus stepped in. In this moment, the old began to pass away and the new was being made.

As Sarah's passionate cries turned to quiet sobs, the Lord imprinted a new picture deep within her spirit, and hope began to gain momentum as His reality became hers. Through such despairing pain and hurt, Christ was weeping too. Sarah describes the transformation that began to take place that day:

> I saw this picture of Jesus kneeling right next to me and He was weeping and hurting so much. I saw how hard it was for Him to see me going through such agony. He was feeling my pain as He watched His daughter suffer. It was almost like He was in more pain than I was and He was carrying the weight of those burdens so much more. Right in that moment, I began to understand that there was a very good reason why I was going through this.
>
> I understood that my heavenly Father wasn't saying "no"; but instead He was saying, "Not yet, My

daughter." God then began to break the bondage that was holding me and I knew this would bring Him glory. I didn't know how that would be, but I knew it would be good!

From that point on things began to change. Yes, there were still struggles but the tight grip of hopelessness was lost. After a year and half of tests, procedures, and surgeries, Sarah was diagnosed with postural orthostatic tachycardia syndrome, also known as POTS. However, as the Enemy loves to revisit defeat, she was told once again that nothing could be done. Still pressing for answers, a search continued for treatment and a response came. This time, the diagnosis had a solution.

ACM, Arnold-Chiari malformation, was the conclusion. The symptoms that Sarah was experiencing were caused by a spinal canal that was too narrow, which squeezed her brain at the bottom of her skull and blocked the necessary flow of vertebral fluid. Brain surgery was the only option but it was an option with promise. During Sarah's junior year of high school, the operation was successful and took away every symptom except the burning sensation.

Today, Sarah still deals with pain but she's able to function. If you were to meet her face-to-face, you wouldn't recognize this struggle. Radiance bursts through her that can only be described as supernatural. A peaceful rest comforts her every day, as God overwhelms her with a strength that proclaims victory over defeat. Is there still struggle? Yes. Do questions still arise? Yes. There's still a hope that someday all pain will be gone, but as Sarah concludes, "I've come so far from where I was."

She has surrendered.

LESSONS LEARNED

Going through such traumatic events, it would seem life had lost its sweet taste for both Ruby and Sarah. However, God has taken their journeys and formed a goodness that's hard to fathom by simple human understanding. The Lord has this wonderful way of working everything together for the good of those who have been called according to His purpose (see Rom. 8:28).

This amazing and almost incomprehensible truth lays the foundation for what each of these women experience on a daily basis. Surrender has opened a door of intimacy with the Almighty that the world finds hard to comprehend. By walking their individual roads, God has given them much wisdom to offer those who need encouragement and, truthfully, we all need such blessed assurance.

With that in mind, I thought it might be good for them to share, in their own words, what they've learned on their journey of surrender in suffering.

Ruby says:

> I've learned that suffering is a critical part of life. It's the bitter that makes the sweet so precious and so wonderful. Suffering may not taste very good in the middle, and certainly spoonfuls of it are hard to choke down; but in the end, there will be this beautiful, wonderful product that is rich and tasteful beyond anything that I can imagine. It's so difficult to find words to describe God's faithfulness.
>
> In my personal experience, there's not a word big enough to describe it. The best way I know to

describe God's faithfulness is to say it comes to me in undeserved measure. God keeps His promises. He offers strength when I am weak. He calms my fears. His love matches no other. He is faithful.

Sarah says:

I've learned there's a sweetness to suffering; and I don't think I would have ever learned it had I not gone through what I've experienced, or what I go through on a daily basis. There is sweetness to getting up in the morning and realizing I cannot go on without my heavenly Father. There's no greater joy than that—knowing He has to work through you for you to get through the day.

There are times when I've felt lonely or rejected, but He has always shown up. He has never let my foot slip; He has never let me turn away. He's always faithful. And quite honestly, I feel like I've seen His faithfulness more in the bad times, more in the suffering, because I have no choice but to cry in His arms.

I should not be able to function, but the Lord has healed me enough to where, despite the pain, I am still able to function. That's a miracle and I just praise the Lord for that every day. It may hurt, but I can dance! It may hurt, but I can run!

The Lord saves those who are crushed in spirit. He's close to the brokenhearted. His power is made strong in our weakness.

God is good. He is good all the time and He is always faithful.

THERE IS HOPE

When we come to white water that's too difficult to navigate and we feel as if we're going to faint as we work to muster the strength to continue on, we must anchor ourselves to our Guide. God knew when He created us what was coming our way, and He has made a provision for us to survive. It's not just for the sake of living but to thrive in a connection with Him through a relationship that identifies with the sufferings of Christ. This is a rare trust indeed.

If you're in an extreme time of grief, pain, and suffering, I share this with you from the depths of my being. The paradox of pain is hard to grasp as a child of God. Making sense of it won't always be possible and, in the midst of the struggle, the purpose won't always be clear. But allow this truth to resonate: God cares for you more deeply than earthly words can communicate. Second Corinthians 1:3–4 says, "Blessed be the God and Father of our Lord Jesus Christ, the Father of mercies and God of all comfort, who comforts us in all our affliction." Our loving, gracious, and compassionate God is crying with you. He is holding you and He is beckoning you to come into His rest. May you be overwhelmed by His love, His peace, His comfort, His strength, and His leading.

When we have faith in Him who is able to do more than we can comprehend, the impossible occurs. God takes what could be harmful and makes a vibrant life of testimony that He uses in powerful ways. He works in the miraculous through our hurt and we find the truth stated in Genesis 50:20: "You intended to harm me, but God intended it all for good" (NLT).

Surrender in suffering offers life in the midst of despair.

TEN

THE END IS THE BEGINNING

The words from our guide were so encouraging. "You made it, man. I wasn't sure what was going to happen, but you made it."

We had finished the course.

As we pulled our raft out of the water and removed our helmets and life jackets, my eyes remained fixed on the river. My heart was still racing; I could feel its steady pulse. My arms felt like noodles and my legs felt ready to give way at a moment's notice. This adventure was coming to a close and as I stood there looking at water that, just minutes earlier, had terrified me to my core, the strangest feeling swept through my soul. I was actually going to miss what we had all just journeyed through.

As I stood on the riverbank, alive, triumphant, and fueled with adrenaline, the shadows had been lifted and my outlook was different. The guide no longer seemed so alarming and scary. The river didn't seem so perilous. During our adventure, not only had I witnessed amazing feats of teamwork, coupled with superior navigational coaching and direction, but I'd been placed right in the middle of the action and had become an integral part of the victory we were experiencing.

There had come a point on the river when I realized I was becoming more of a hindrance than support. My constant complaining, incessant whines, bitter comments, and insistence on doing things my own way were only causing grief for me and everyone who was with me. The concept of unity was all but lost as I sought to maintain control.

Somewhere along the way, I'd decided enough was enough and I needed to let go and trust. I needed to surrender. For me to be fully effective in the role I was to play aboard the raft, absolute surrender was necessary and had to become my focus. I had to abandon what I thought was best in order to follow the lead of the one who really knew what was best.

When it comes to the waters of our spiritual lives, we have a choice. We can choose to be led by our pride of self, which only enables us to trust what we can see. This binds us to an earthly decay. Our spiritual fervor and discipline slowly fade as our purpose is never truly fulfilled. That not only causes negative consequences for us, but also for those in our realm of influence because we hinder and even stop God's movement in our lives. This negativity affects His movement through us into others, and corrupts the flow into the next generation. We aren't pouring forth rivers of living water but rather sweeping dust from dried streams. Water brings nourishment; dust chokes the very air we breathe.

Our other option is to surrender and fully accept God's authority over our lives. Our way equals brokenness and an unfulfilled design. However, God's way provides unparalleled restoration that rebuilds our lives for the purpose of our creation. No amount of earthly wealth and work will bring that kind of satisfaction. We'll always be looking for ways to keep climbing the ladder. We'll never become truly settled because the appetite of our self-worth is a black hole that can never be filled.

It's easy to get caught up in the here and now and contain our treasures in an earthly vessel. However, the purpose of surrender on this earth is not for mere success in a world that won't be around forever, but for the purpose of God's glory set for all eternity. Life abundant doesn't mean luxury in excess. Christ calls us to set our eyes on the heavenly prize. He says, "Don't store up treasures here on earth, where moths eat them and rust destroys them, and where thieves break in and steal. Store your treasures in heaven, where moths and rust cannot destroy, and thieves do not break in and steal" (Matt. 6:19–20, NLT).

Paul encourages us with these words: "But I press on to possess that perfection for which Christ Jesus first possessed me. No, dear brothers and sisters, I have not achieved it, but I focus on this one thing: Forgetting the past and looking forward to what lies ahead, I press on to reach the end of the race and receive the heavenly prize for which God, through Christ Jesus, is calling us" (Phil. 3:12–14, NLT).

Our best life is ahead of us when we're not solely earthbound. Take this truth into strong consideration and ask yourself where you keep your treasure. Where is your storehouse? What future are you looking toward? Remember, "For where your treasure is, there your heart will be also" (Matt. 6:21, NIV).

SEEK GOD AND LIVE

Seek the LORD and live.

Amos 5:6, NIV

God longs to see devotion deeply developed within you and me so that we may be intimately linked and guided by Him. Yes, He is a jealous God, but not in the typical way we view jealousy (see Exod. 34:14). His is of divine nature, not darkened and tainted by sin. It's of the purest kind and is a benefit to us, not a hindrance. It's driven by His love for us as His dear children and creation. He desires that His perfect nature would obliterate our sinful nature so that we may be fully effective in His created purpose, pouring streams of living water even after we've left this earth. His power within us is what makes our lives great.

What greater joy can there really be? The Creator of the entire universe, whose sovereignty rules over every living thing, wants to use us as vessels so that we, with great assurance, fully rise up to be all He made us to be. He wants to not only help us get there, but pour His power into us so that we'll absolutely reach that goal. In order for that to be a reality, our lives *must* end to really begin. As my friend Dr. Jim DeLoach says, "Find your heart. Focus your heart. Surrender your heart."

Scripture gives the greatest picture of what it means to "seek the LORD and live." After all, that's what true surrender is all about. I want to encourage you to strive to live this life. It's here that we find true and lasting joy because "we have this treasure in jars of clay to show that this all-surpassing power is from God and not from us" (2 Cor. 4:7, NIV).

By His power alone, we can be a light to a darkened world and live out these commands: "Therefore be imitators of God, as beloved children; and walk in love, just as Christ also loved you and gave Himself up for us, an offering and a sacrifice to God as a fragrant aroma.... Do not participate in the unfruitful deeds of darkness.... Therefore be careful how you walk, not as unwise men but as wise, making the most of your time" (Eph. 5:1–2, 11, 15–16).

In living this way, we can reveal the all-surpassing greatness of God to a dying world as we stand confident and strong in any circumstance that we encounter. As we focus our heart in surrender to our Creator and King, our eyes will see beyond our limitations. And we will find that fear, whatever way it may come about, will not be a dominant influence.

SURRENDER

Life really is like a river and, as believers, we have Christ as our Guide. No matter the type of waters ahead—calm and serene, or white peaks and raging—Jesus is at the center of it all. Not only does He give direction, but when we take matters into our own hands and catapult overboard because of our stubbornness, He's there standing on the water that rushes over our heads, able to pull us to our feet so we can stand with Him and walk on the water victoriously. As God's creation, we have our limits, but He has every capability to lead us beyond our restricted state. Surrender is key as we maintain focus on Him, eyes and ears locked on the Giver of life.

Hebrews says, "Now the God of peace, who brought up from the dead the great Shepherd of the sheep through the blood of the eternal covenant, even Jesus our Lord, equip you in every good thing to do His will, working in us that which is pleasing in His sight, through Jesus Christ, to whom be the glory forever and ever. Amen" (Heb. 13:20–21). Journey the river wild and make it count! You won't drown, your raft won't split in two, and in the end, you'll stand on the riverbank in triumphant glory, eagerly ready to cross to the other side. Surrender doesn't bring loss, but gain. It's quite amazing!

Grace and peace to you.

EPILOGUE

KNOWING JESUS

As a parent, you sometimes have conversations that you never really thought you'd ever end up having. One such conversation occurred the other night. I walked upstairs to my daughter's room and could barely walk into the room because there were so many stuffed animals, blankets, and toys covering her floor. *Time to clean up*, I thought. So I called her upstairs. She came right up to the door leading into her room and stopped in the doorway. "Sweetie, it's time to clean up your room," I said.

"Why?" she asked.

"Well, take a look around. There's hardly any walking space. We need to pick up everything that's lying on the floor," I stated.

"Daddy," she said, "you caaaaann walk around."

"I'm having a hard time doing that, Bit, because there's stuff all over the floor," I said.

"No there's not," she stated, rather sure of her own truth.

"Sweetie," I said, working on a patient response. "You can clearly see all the stuffed animals, toys, and blankets everywhere, right?" I asked.

"Yes," she answered.

"Then why are you telling me that there's 'nothing' on the floor?" I questioned, now quite curious as to what her answer would be.

"'Cause I don't want there to be," she stated quickly with rather strong conviction in her tone.

"Okay," I answered, "but that doesn't solve the problem of the fact that there is still stuff all over your floor."

She took another look, and then looked at me. "But Daaaaad," she said, after thinking for a second. "I really don't want there to be anything on my floor, because I don't want to clean it up."

I quietly chuckled and a slight smile formed on my face. I loved her honesty. "Yeah, I understand that," I said. "But the truth is, there's a mess here that needs to be cleaned up, and just because you may not want it to be true and you don't like the truth, doesn't mean it isn't true."

She contemplated my answer and then bent down and picked up a stuffed animal. "Okay," she said. "I guess I'll start here, with this one . . . but this is going to take forever." Then she exclaimed, "How'd this room get so messy anyways?!" And we began the process of cleaning up.

Have you ever heard the phrase, "The truth can be hard to admit"? It really can be. In a time where social media has such a strong impact and the opinions of our peers and global influencers are stated rather emphatically, it can be easy to sway in the direction of opinion rather than truth. The reality of why every human needs a Savior can be hard to accept, but truth doesn't change because a mere thought or opinion that says, "I just don't like it that way."

Man is a sinner. We're not born as perfect beings; we mess up, and we mess up a lot. As a parent, it's a daily task to teach my children righteousness and goodness. I didn't have to teach my daughter how to stand in her doorway and lie when the truth was right in front of her. I've never had to teach my son how to talk back; and I've never had to teach my children how to scream at one another, hit each other, show unkindness, or be self-serving and selfish. That comes naturally.

However, I have had to teach them how *not to*. I've had to teach them behaviors of goodness. They're not naturally inclined toward such things. That can be hard to admit, but it's the truth. Children misbehave, naturally. We've all been children, and thus, we've also had that problem. The problem doesn't go away as we move into adulthood either. And that problem has a name; it's called *sin*.

Every man has been given a conscience, an innate discerning of right and wrong. But people mess up and make bad choices; otherwise, laws would be pointless. The human race has had to put a system in place that provides consequences for our actions. A system measured by a standard of right and wrong that says, "These actions are not good."

Spiritually, for our souls, our Creator also holds us to a standard—but His standard is absolute perfection, which is completely unattainable, no matter how much we want to disagree. And our Creator God has revealed the truth of the "why" and He tells us in His Word. It's because man is a sinner. Romans

3:23 says, "For everyone has sinned; we all fall short of God's glorious standard" (NLT).

Though we may find that hard to admit, and though we may not want it to be true, the truth still stands. It doesn't change. This thing called *sin* separates us from God, and no amount of work we try to do—even works based upon *good nature*—won't solve the problem. There's still a mess that needs to be cleaned up.

A plan of redemption must take place; otherwise we remain separated from God even in death. A full separation from God in death is an eternal separation, and will bind those who have been separated to a destination called hell. But, thankfully, a plan of redemption is in place and the story doesn't end there; it keeps going!

John 3:16 says, "For this is how God loved the world: He gave his one and only Son, so that everyone who believes in him will not perish but have eternal life" (NLT). God is love. I'm talking *real* love. He is patient, He is kind, He is not proud or rude. He is always hopeful, He never gives up, and He completely endures. Though His standard of perfection is very real, so is His love and hope for you and me—so much so that He gave us the gift of His one and only Son, Jesus.

Jesus came to the earth as a baby. He lived as fully man and fully God. However, He did something that we, as a fallen creation, are unable to do. Jesus lived a perfect, sinless life and then willingly took the blame of our sin upon Himself. By doing this, forgiveness was graciously provisioned by God because of the sacrifice of Jesus. And by His grace we can be saved. He did this to take the punishment of our sin away from us, to remove the dreadful destination of hell from our eternal existence, and to close the separation between God and us.

Sin is a costly thing, and it has put a price on our heads. The wages of sin is death (see Rom. 6:23). So Christ took it upon Himself and died a truly excruciating death on a cross for us. But then three days later, He was raised again—defeating death, proving the fact that He was God, and providing a way to victory for us in life eternal. Talk about real love!

And as John 3:16 states, salvation comes to us by believing in Jesus, by accepting the truth that we are sinners, and by fully trusting that Jesus Christ is who He says He is. First John 5:12 tells us, "He who has the Son has the life; he who does not have the Son of God does not have the life."

Our salvation relies totally on Jesus and His grace alone. We cannot work to earn it, because He already accomplished the work. And because Christ completed the work, the gift of salvation is free for us (see Rom. 6:23). Literally, it is free! Thus, our faith in Christ determines our destiny, for it is by grace through faith that we are saved (see Eph. 2:8-9).

Surrender starts here, in the free gift of salvation. Being able to accept this truth really does bring freedom. It is life-giving! If you have not received Christ as your Savior and made a personal commitment to Him, you have a chance to do so. Don't let it slip by!

To receive Christ as your personal Savior, you can say a simple prayer of acknowledgment, a prayer where you personally recognize your own sinfulness, accept the forgiveness of Christ, and place your faith in Him alone for salvation. This truth defines what will happen to you in eternity. Though it may be hard to admit and understand at first, it is real.

The prayer can be something like this if you need guidance:

> I believe that You, Jesus, are the Son of God. I believe that You died on the cross for my sin and that you arose from the grave and conquered death. I acknowledge that I am a sinner, and I ask for Your forgiveness of my sins. Be my Savior and my Lord. I place my faith in You alone for my salvation. Guide and lead me to obey what you teach and what you command in your Word and through my life. Provide others who will help me along this new path. Thank you for giving me life and saving me from death. Amen.

If you did pray that prayer, congratulations and welcome to the family!

Finding a Bible-believing and -teaching church home will be very important for you on this new path. Begin to seek out and find that kind of community, because inside that framework you can grow in this new journey with Christ. Within that church family, speak with a pastor about the importance of raising your flag for Christ through the action of baptism.

For those who are still curious and feel like you're just not sure, please know this: Surrendering to Jesus is such a wonderful thing. I hope that soon you are willing and ready to step into the amazing family of God and unite fully with your Creator. Surrender. The abundant gifts of joy, hope, and life are here.

Grace and peace to you.

NOTES

PROLOGUE

1. Hampton J. Keathley III, "The Unity of the Spirit," Bible. org, published May 21, 2004, https://bible.org/article/ unity-spirit-ephesians-41-6.

CHAPTER 2

1. Dr. Spiros Zodhiates and Dr. Warren Patrick Baker, eds., *The Hebrew-Greek Key Word Study Bible: NASB-77 Edition* (Chattanooga, TN: AMG Publishers, 2008), 2220.

CHAPTER 3

1. Zodhiates and Baker, eds., 1901.

CHAPTER 4

1. Charles Spurgeon, "Shut Your Eyes to Sin," August 5 in *At the Master's Feet* (Grand Rapids, MI: Zondervan, 2005).

2. Oswald Chambers, quoted in "Joy" in *The Quotable Oswald Chambers* (Grand Rapids, MI: Discovery House Publishers, 2008).

3. Dr. Spiros Zodhiates and Dr. Warren Patrick Baker, eds., *The Hebrew-Greek Key Word Study Bible: NASB-77 Edition* (Chattanooga, TN: AMG Publishers, 2008), 336.

4. Tim Keller, quoted in "26 Quotes About Idolatry," ChristianQuotes.info, accessed February 9, 2018, https://www.christianquotes.info/quotes-by-topic/quotes-about-idolatry/#axzz56dOHpS00.

CHAPTER 5

1. Dr. Spiros Zodhiates and Dr. Warren Patrick Baker, eds., *The Hebrew-Greek Key Word Study Bible: NASB-77 Edition* (Chattanooga, TN: AMG Publishers, 2008), 752.

2. Edward Mote, "My Hope is Built on Nothing Less," Hymnal.net, accessed February 9, 2018, https://www.hymnal.net/en/hymn/h/298.

CHAPTER 6

1. Andrew Murray, *With Christ in the School of Prayer* (New York: Fleming H. Revell Company), 170.

2. George MacDonald, quoted in Warren W. Wiersbe, *Be Determined: Standing Firm in the Face of Opposition* (Colorado Springs, CO: David C. Cook, 1992), 23.

3. Oswald Chambers, quoted in "Oswald Chambers Quotes," Goodreads, accessed February 9, 2018, https://www.goodreads.com/quotes/166479-we-tend-to-use-prayer-as-a-last-resort-but.

CHAPTER 8

1. "Ancient Hebrew Social Hierarchy," Hierarchy Structure, accessed October 11, 2017, https://www.hierarchystructure.com/ancient-hebrew-social-hierarchy/.

2. "Given Names, Judaism, and Jewish History," The Given Names Databases, accessed October 11, 2017, https://www.jewishgen.org/databases/GivenNames/ancient.htm.

3. "Ancient Hebrew Social Hierarchy," Hierarchy Structure, accessed October 11, 2017, https://www.hierarchystructure.com/ancient-hebrew-social-hierarchy/.

4. "History: Social Structure of Ancient Israel," Encyclopedia.com, accessed February 9, 2018, http://www.encyclopedia.com/religion/encyclopedias-almanacs-transcripts-and-maps/history-social-structure-ancient-israel#National_Class_Structure.

5. "Ancient Hebrew Social Hierarchy," Hierarchy Structure, accessed October 11, 2017, https://www.hierarchystructure.com/ancient-hebrew-social-hierarchy/.

6. "History: Social Structure of Ancient Israel," Encyclopedia.com, accessed February 9, 2018, http://www.encyclopedia.com/religion/encyclopedias-almanacs-transcripts-and-maps/history-social-structure-ancient-israel#National_Class_Structure.

7. Warren W. Wiersbe, *Be Concerned: Making a Difference in Your Lifetime* (Colorado Springs, CO: David C. Cook, 1996), 32.

8. Wiersbe, 33.

PUBLICATIONS

Fort Washington, PA 19034

This book is published by CLC Publications, an outreach of CLC Ministries International. The purpose of CLC is to make evangelical Christian literature available to all nations so that people may come to faith and maturity in the Lord Jesus Christ. We hope this book has been life changing and has enriched your walk with God through the work of the Holy Spirit. If you would like to know more about CLC, we invite you to visit our website:

www.clcusa.org

To know more about the remarkable story of the founding of CLC International we encourage you to read

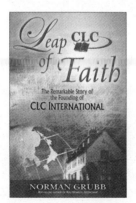

LEAP OF FAITH

Norman Grubb

Paperback
Size 5¹/₄ x 8, Pages 248
ISBN: 978-0-87508-650-7
ISBN (*e-book*): 978-1-61958-055-8